PIANO • VOCAL • GUITAR

# THE BIG BOOK OF

# FOLKSONGS

ISBN 978-1-4584-2115-9

HAL•LEONARD®
CORPORATION
7777 W. BLUEMOUND RD. P.O. BOX 13819 MILWAUKEE, WI 53213

In Australia Contact:
**Hal Leonard Australia Pty. Ltd.**
4 Lentara Court
Cheltenham, Victoria, 3192 Australia
Email: ausadmin@halleonard.com.au

Visit Hal Leonard Online at
**www.halleonard.com**

# CONTENTS

# ALL NIGHT, ALL DAY

Traditional Spiritual

Day is dy-in' in ___ the west,
Now I lay me down ___ to sleep,

an-gels watch-in' o-ver me, my Lord. ___ Sleep, my child, and
an-gels watch-in' o-ver me, my Lord. ___ Pray the Lord my

take ___ your rest, an-gels watch-in' o-ver me.
soul ___ to keep, an-gels watch-in' o-ver me.

# ALL THE PRETTY LITTLE HORSES

Southeastern American Folksong

**Gently rocking**

Hush-you-bye, don't you cry, go to sleep-y, lit-tle ba - by. When you wake, you shall have all the pret-ty lit-tle hors - es. Blacks and bays, dap-ples and greys, coach and six-a-lit-tle hors - es. Hush-you-bye, don't you cry, go to sleep-y, lit-tle ba - by.

# AND THE GREEN GRASS GROWS ALL AROUND

Traditional

*Additional Lyrics*

6. And in that egg there was a bird
   The prettiest bird that you ever did see
   Now the bird in the egg...

7. And on that bird there was a wing
   The prettiest wing that you ever did see
   Now the wing on the bird...

8. And on that wing there was a feather
   The prettiest feather that you ever did see
   Now the feather on the wing...

9. And on that feather there was a bug
   The prettiest bug that you ever did see
   Now the bug on the feather...

10. And on that bug there was a germ
    The prettiest germ that you ever did see
    Now the germ on the bug...

# ANIMAL FAIR

American Folksong

I went to the an-i-mal fair, _____ the birds and the beasts were there. _____ The big ba-boon by the light of the moon was comb-ing his au-burn hair. _____ You

# ANNABEL LEE

Music Anonymous
Words based on a poem by EDGAR ALLAN POE

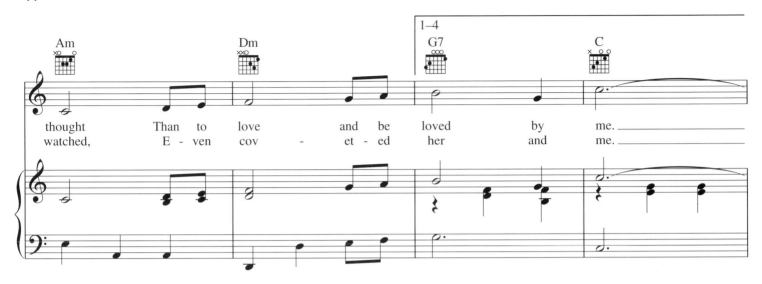

thought      Than  to   love          and  be   loved        by    me.____
watched,     E  -  ven  cov   -   et  -  ed  her        and    me.____

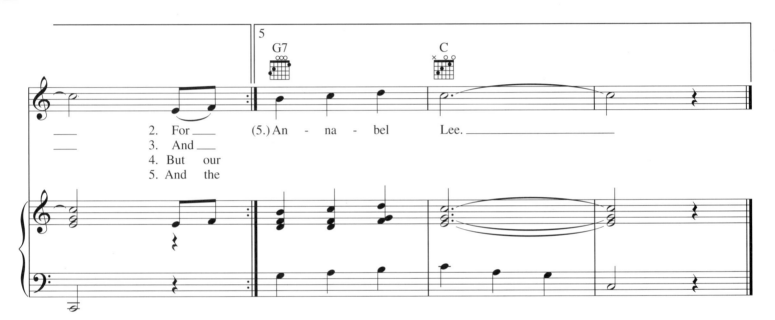

____  2.  For ____   (5.) An  -  na  -  bel   Lee. ____
____  3.  And ____
      4.  But  our
      5.  And  the

*Additional Lyrics*

3.  And this is the reason that long, long ago,
    In this kingdom by the sea,
    There arose a strong wind blowing out of a cloud,
    Chilled and killed my dear Annabel Lee.
    And her highborn kinsmen, they quickly came,
    And they bore her away from me.
    And they sealed her remains in a sepulcher deep,
    In this kingdom by the sea.

4.  But our love, it was stronger by far than the love
    Of the ones who were older than we,
    Of the many far older and wiser than we,
    Of those older and wiser than we.
    Ah, but neither angels in sky above,
    Nor the demons beneath the sea,
    Could sever my soul from the soul of my love
    Of my beautiful Annabel Lee.

5.  And the moon never beams without bringing me dreams
    In this kingdom by the sea,
    And the stars never rise but I feel the bright eyes
    Of the beautiful Annabel Lee.
    Through the night I lie by my dearest one,
    By the side of my bride to be,
    Though she lies in her sepulcher silent and cold.
    Oh, my beautiful Annabel Lee.

# THE ASH GROVE

Old Welsh Air

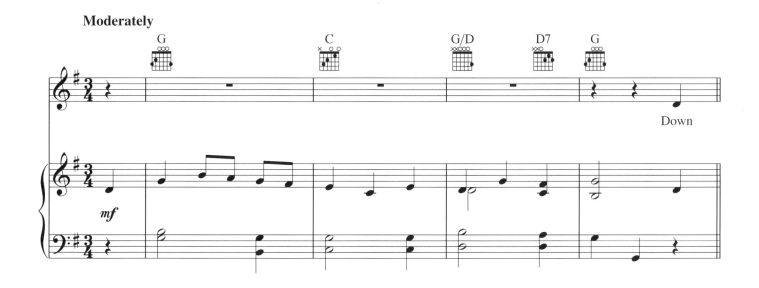

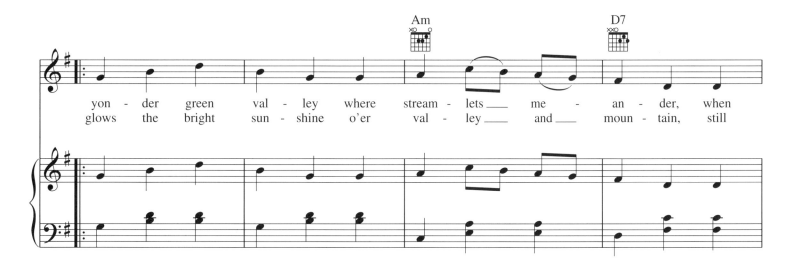

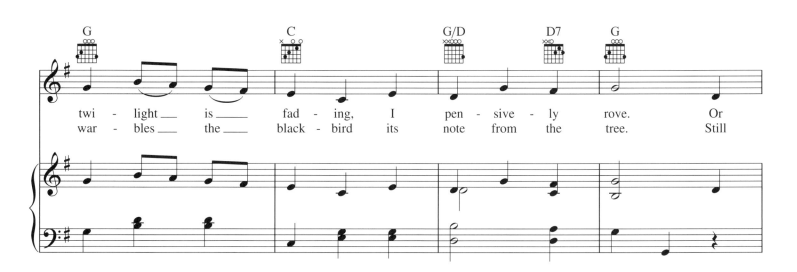

# AU CLAIR DE LA LUNE

French Folksong

**Moderately slow**

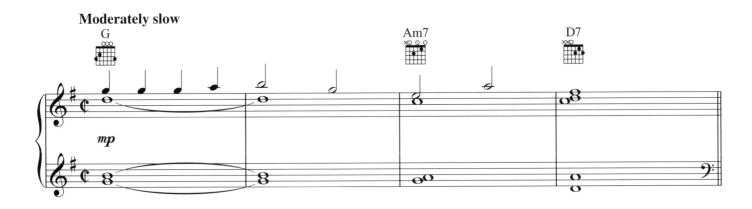

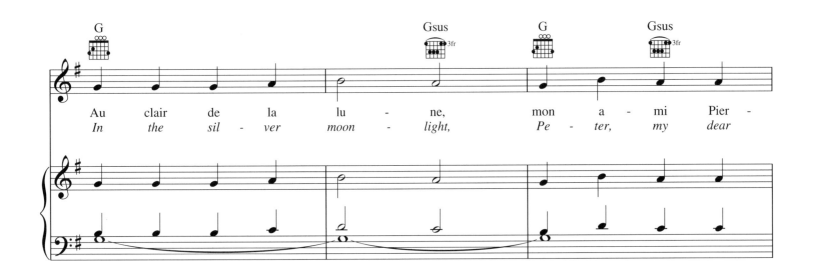

Au clair de la lu - ne, mon a - mi Pier -
*In the sil - ver moon - light, Pe - ter, my dear*

rot, prê - te moi ta plu - me
*friend, please lend me your pen - cil*

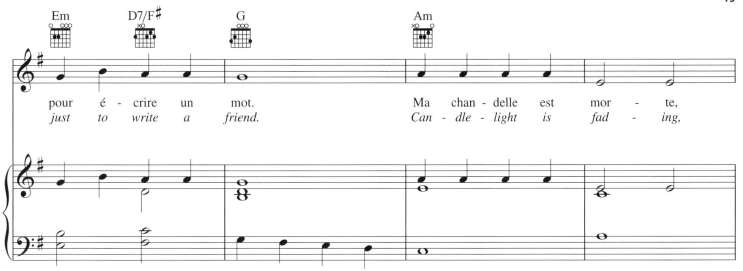

pour é - crire un mot.
*just to write a friend.*
Ma chan - delle est mor - te,
*Can - dle - light is fad - ing,*

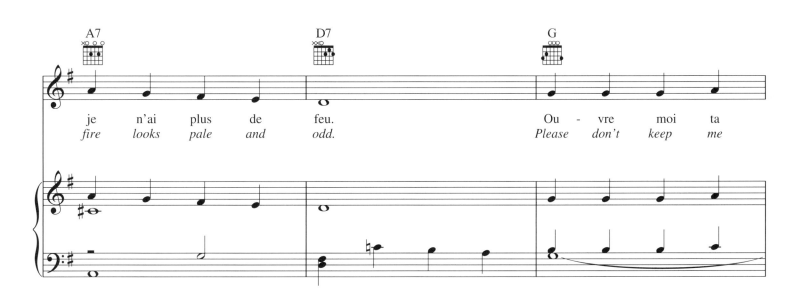

je n'ai plus de feu.
*fire looks pale and odd.*
Ou - vre moi ta
*Please don't keep me*

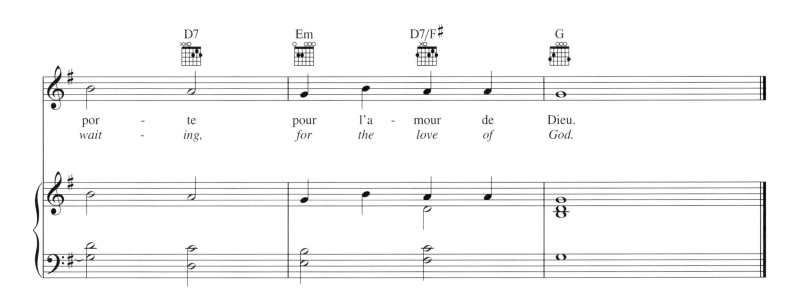

por - te pour l'a - mour de Dieu.
*wait - ing, for the love of God.*

# AUPRÈS DE MA BLONDE
## (Nearby to My Dear One)

French Folksong

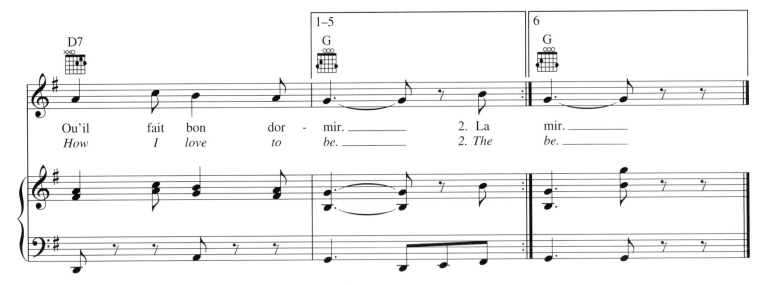

Ou'il   fait   bon   dor - mir._____   2. La   mir._____
*How   I   love   to   be._____   2. The   be._____*

## Additional Lyrics

2. La caill', la tourterelle,
   Et la jolie perdrix
   La caill', la tourterelle,
   Et la jolie perdrix,
   Et ma jolie colombe
   Qui chante jour et nuit.
   *Refrain*

3. Qui chante pour les filles
   Qui n'ont pas de mari,
   Qui chante pour les filles
   Qui n'ont pas de mari.
   Pour moir, ne chante guère,
   Car j'en ai un joli,
   *Refrain*

4. Dites-nous donc, la belle,
   Oú donc est vot' mari?
   Dites-nous donc, la belle,
   Où donc est vot' mari?
   Il est dans la Hollande,
   Les Hollandais l'ont pris,
   *Refrain*

5. Que donneriez-vous, belle,
   Pour avoir votre ami?
   Que donneriez-vous, belle,
   Pour avoir votre ami?
   Je donnerais Versailles,
   Paris et Saint-Denis,
   *Refrain*

6. Je donnerais Versailles,
   Paris et Saint-Denis,
   Je donnerais Versailles,
   Paris et Saint-Denis,
   Les tours de Notre-Dame,
   Et l'clocher d'mon pays;
   *Refrain*

2. *The quail, the grey woodpigeon,*
   *And speckled partridge come,*
   *The quail, the grey woodpigeon,*
   *And speckled partridge come.*
   *My little dove, my dearest,*
   *That night and day doth croon.*
   Refrain

3. *It's comforting the maidens*
   *Unmarried and alone,*
   *It's comforting the maidens,*
   *Unmarried and alone.*
   *Sweet dove, don't sing for me then,*
   *A man, I have my own.*
   Refrain

4. *O tell us, tell us, lady,*
   *Where is your husband gone?*
   *O tell us, tell us, lady,*
   *Where is your husband gone?*
   *In Holland he's a prisoner,*
   *The Dutch have taken him.*
   Refrain

5. *What would you give, my beauty,*
   *To have your husband home?*
   *What would you give, my beauty,*
   *To have your husband home?*
   *Versailles I'd gladly give them*
   *And Paris and Notre Dame.*
   Refrain

6. *Versailles I'd gladly give them,*
   *And Paris and Notre Dame,*
   *Versailles I'd gladly give them,*
   *And Paris and Notre Dame,*
   *Saint Denis's Cathedral,*
   *And our church-spire at home.*
   Refrain

# THE BAMBOO FLUTE

Chinese Folksong

# AURA LEE

Words by W.W. FOSDICK
Music by GEORGE R. POULTON

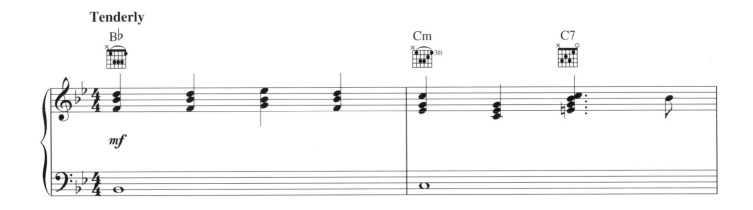

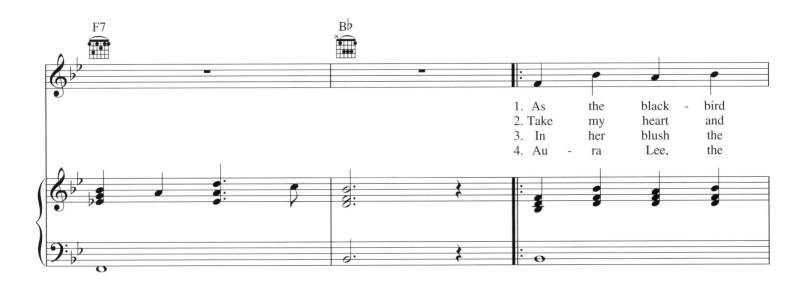

1. As the black - bird
2. Take my heart and
3. In her blush the
4. Au - ra Lee, the

in the spring, 'neath the wil - low tree, ___
take my ring, I give my all to thee. ___
rose was born, 'twas mu - sic when she spake. ___
bird may flee the wil - low's gold - en hair, ___

# THE BANANA BOAT SONG

Jamaican Work Song

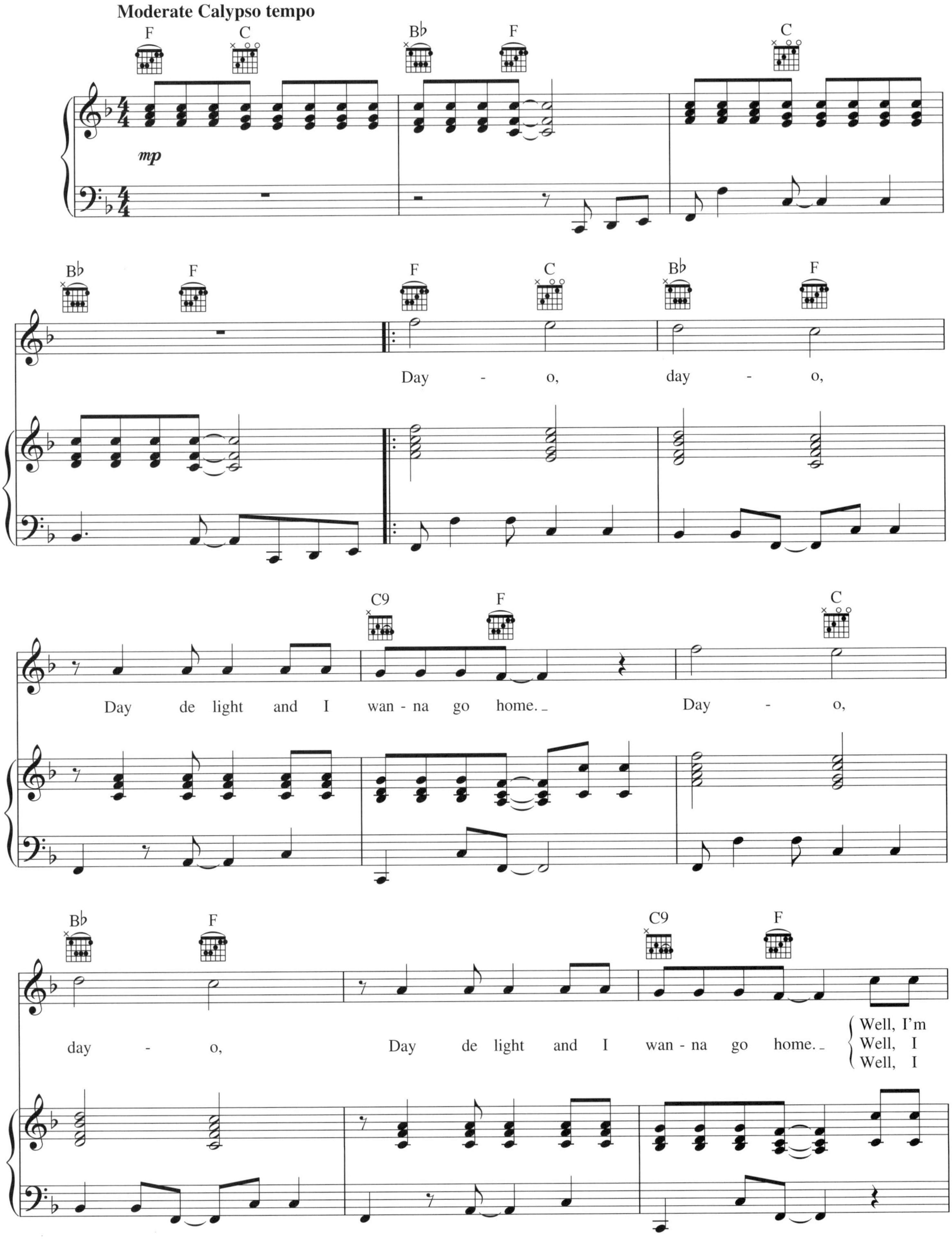

Moderate Calypso tempo
F C Bb F C
mp
Bb F F C Bb F
Day - o, day - o,
C9 F C
Day de light and I wan - na go home. Day - o,
Bb F C9 F
day - o, Day de light and I wan - na go home.
Well, I'm
Well, I
Well, I

load - in' de ba - na - na boats    all  night  long, __
sleep   by   sun    and  I   work   by  moon, __
pack  up  all  my  things  and  I'll  go   to  sea, __

Day    de  light   and  I

wan - na  go  home. __

{ Hey!     all  of  de  work  —  men    sing  this  song. __
{ When  I   get   some  mon  -  ey  gon - na  quit  so  soon. __
 Den  de  ba - na - na's  see __  the     last   of   me. __

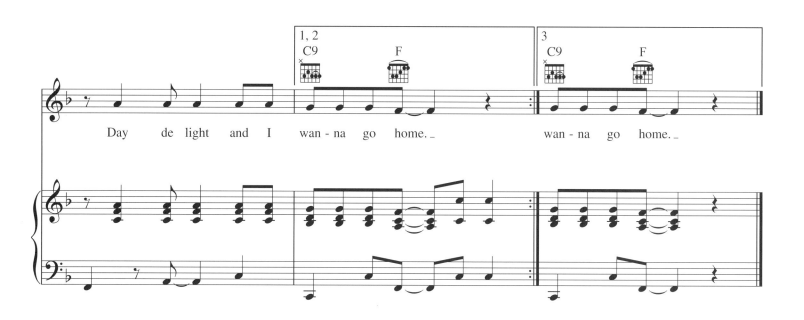

Day    de  light   and  I   wan - na  go  home. __

wan - na  go  home. __

# THE BAND PLAYED ON

Words by JOHN E. PALMER
Music by CHARLES B. WARD

hind the man who was their joy and pride. _____

stayed up - stairs and ex - er - cised his feet. _____

hap - py Mis - sus Ca - sey now for life. _____

**Waltz**

For _____ Ca - sey would waltz with a straw - ber - ry

blonde, and the band played on. _____ He'd

glide 'cross the floor with the girl he a - dored, and the band

# BARBARA ALLEN

Traditional English Folksong

*Additional Lyrics*

3. Then slowly, slowly she came up,
   And slowly she came nigh him,
   And all she said when there she came,
   "Young man, I think you're dying."

4. As she was walking o'er the fields,
   She heard the deadbell knellin',
   And every stroke the deadbell gave
   Cried, "Woe to Barb'ra Allen!"

5. When he was dead and laid in grave,
   Her heart was struck with sorrow,
   "O mother, mother, make my bed,
   For I shall die tomorrow."

6. "Farewell," she said, "ye virgins all,
   And shun the fault I fell in.
   Henceforth take warning by the fall
   Of cruel Barb'ra Allen."

# BENDEMEER'S STREAM

Words by THOMAS MOORE
Traditional Irish Folk Melody

# BILLY BOY

Traditional

*Additional Lyrics*

3. Did she set you a chair,
   Billy Boy, Billy Boy?
   Did she set you a chair,
   Tell me, Billy.
   Yes, she set for me a chair,
   She has ringlets in her hair,
   She's a young thing,
   And cannot leave her mother.

4. Can she bake cherry pie,
   Billy Boy, Billy Boy?
   Can she bake cherry pie,
   Tell me, Billy.
   She can bake a cherry pie,
   There's a twinkle in her eye,
   She's a young thing,
   And cannot leave her mother.

# BLOW THE MAN DOWN

Traditional Sea Chantey

# BLOW THE CANDLES OUT

American Folksong

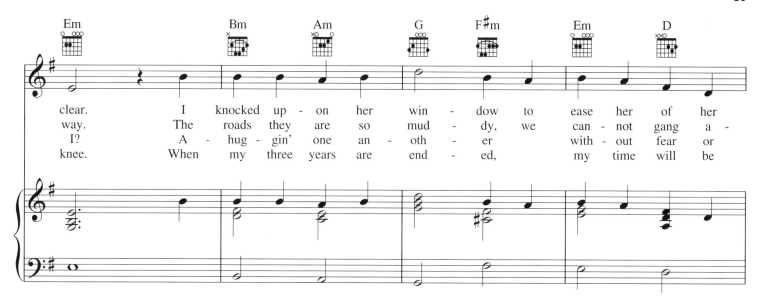

clear.    I knocked up - on her win - dow to ease her of her
way. The roads they are so mud - dy, we can - not gang a -
I? A - hug - gin' one an - oth - er with - out fear or
knee. When my three years are end - ed, my time will be

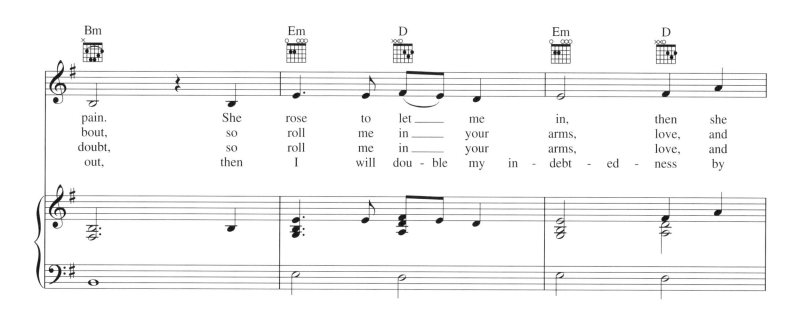

pain.    She rose to let _____ me in, then she
bout, so roll me in _____ your arms, love, and
doubt, so roll me in _____ your arms, love, and
out, then I will dou - ble my in - debt - ed - ness by

barred the door a - gain.    I blow - ing the can - dles out.
blow the can - dles out. Your
blow the can - dles out. And

# BLOW THE WIND SOUTHERLY

Traditional English Folksong

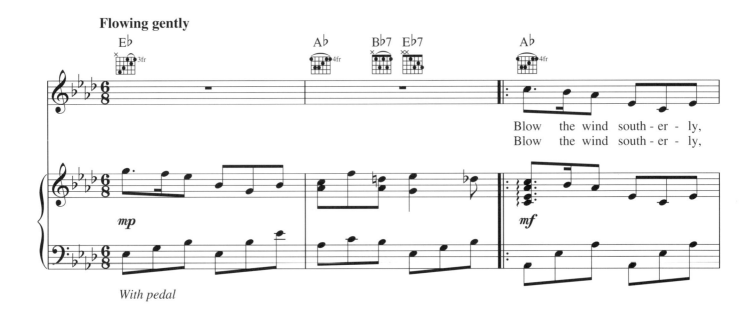

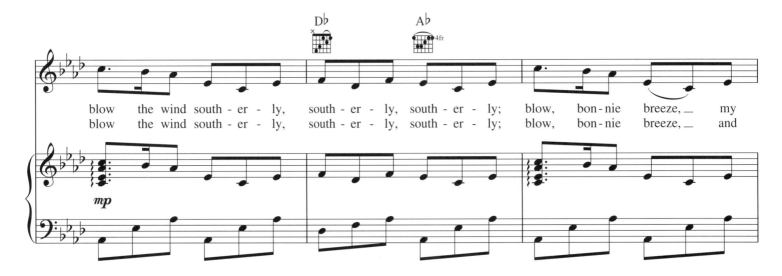

# BOIL THEM CABBAGE DOWN

American Folksong

# CA' THE YOWES

Words by ROBERT BURNS
Old Scottish Melody

1., 4. Ca'  the yowes  to  the knowes,  ca' them whaur the
2. Hark,  the ma - vis  to  eve - ning sang,  sound - ing Clu - den's
3. Fair  and love - ly  as  thou art,  thou  hast stol'n  my

hea - ther grows,  ca' them whaur the burn - ie rows,
woods a - mang;  then  a fauld - ing let us gang,
ver - y heart;  I  can die but can - na part,

my  bon - nie dear - ie.  my  bon - nie dear - ie.
my  bon - nie dear - ie.
my  bon - nie dear - ie.

# THE BOLL WEEVIL

Texas Folksong, c. 1890

# CINDY

Southern Appalachian Folksong

# COME ALL YE FAIR AND TENDER MAIDENS

Kentucky Folksong

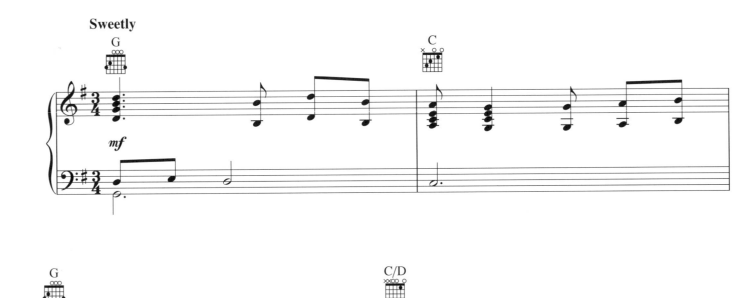

1. Come all ye

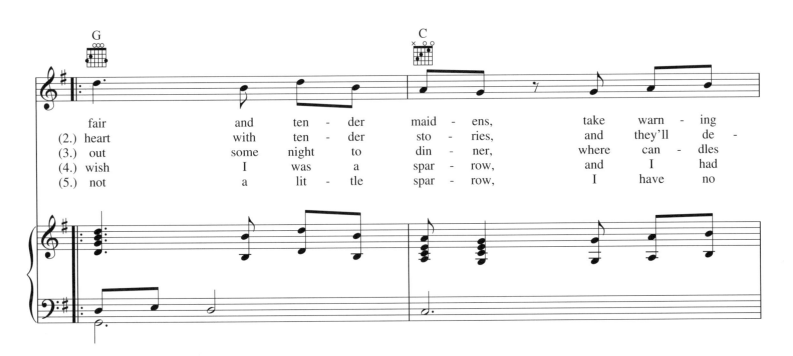

| | | | | | | |
|---|---|---|---|---|---|---|
| fair | and | ten- | der | maid- | ens, | take warn- ing |
| (2.) heart | with | ten- | der | sto- | ries, | and they'll de- |
| (3.) out | some | night | to | din- | ner, | where can- dles |
| (4.) wish | I | was | a | spar- | row, | and I had |
| (5.) not | a | lit- | tle | spar- | row, | I have no |

*Additional Lyrics*

6. Come all ye fair and tender maidens,
   Take warning how you court young men.
   One night they may shine like stars above you,
   To love you that night–but ne'er again.

7. If I had known, before he courted,
   That love was such a killing thing,
   I'd a-locked my heart in a chest of iron,
   And tied it down so it couldn't take wing.

# COTTON EYED JOE

Tennessee Folksong

**Wistfully**

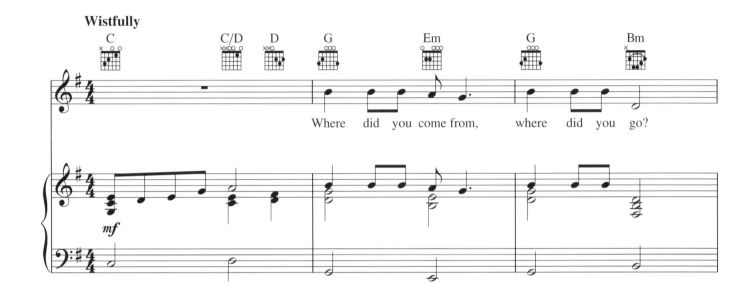

Where did you come from, where did you go?

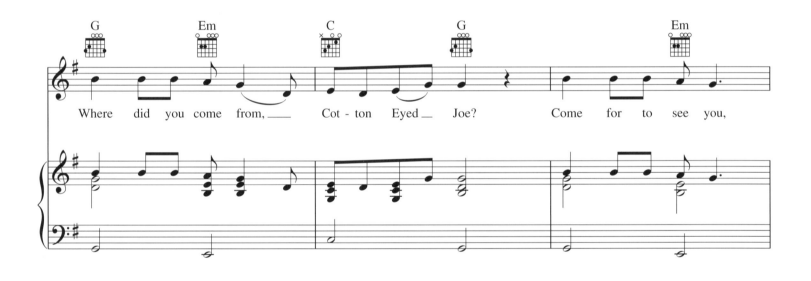

Where did you come from, ___ Cot-ton Eyed ___ Joe? Come for to see you,

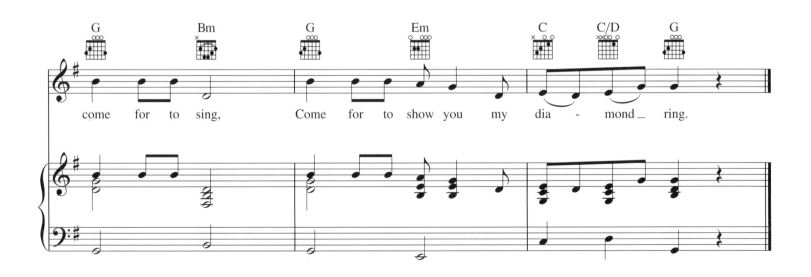

come for to sing, Come for to show you my dia-mond ___ ring.

# DIDN'T MY LORD DELIVER DANIEL?

African-American Spiritual

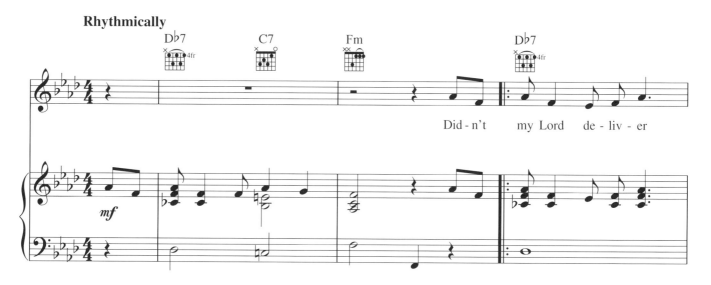

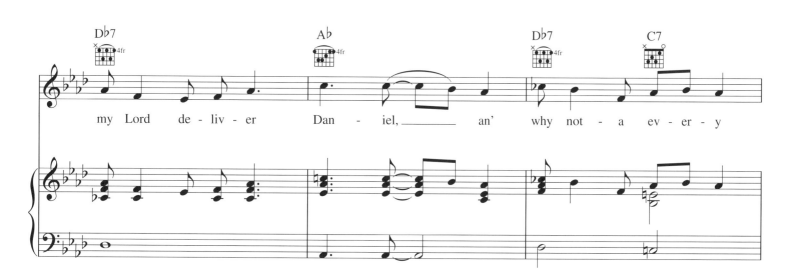

# COUNTRY GARDENS

Traditional

# THE CRUEL WAR IS RAGING

American Folksong

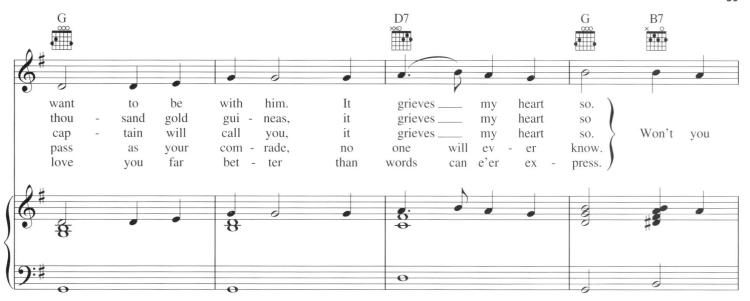

want      to    be    with    him.    It    grieves ___ my    heart    so.
thou - sand    gold    gui - neas,    it    grieves ___ my    heart    so.
cap - tain    will    call    you,    it    grieves ___ my    heart    so.
pass    as    your    com - rade,    no    one    will    ev - er    know.
love    you    far    bet - ter    than    words    can    e'er    ex - press.    Won't    you

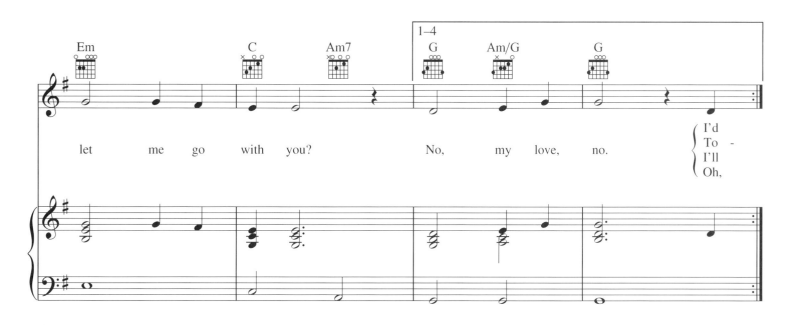

let    me    go    with    you?    No,    my    love,    no.    I'd / To - / I'll / Oh,

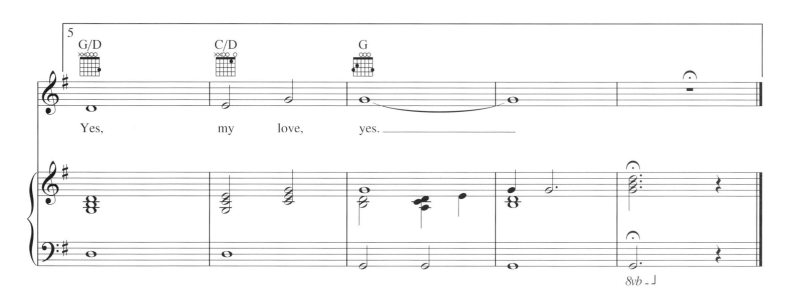

Yes,    my    love,    yes. ___

*8vb*

# (I Wish I Was In)
# DIXIE

Words and Music by
DAN DECATUR EMMETT

# EIN PROSIT DER GEMÜTLICHKEIT

German Drinking Song

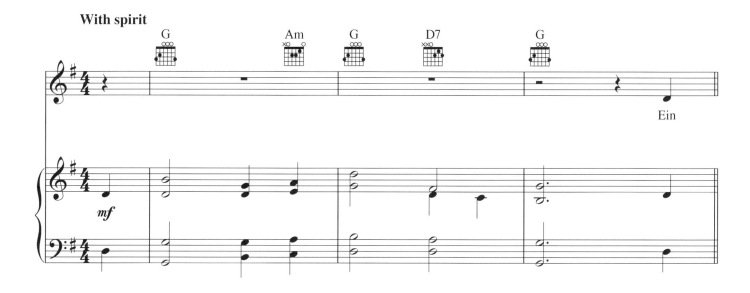

Ein

Pro - sit, ein Pro - sit der Ge - müt - lich - keit, ein

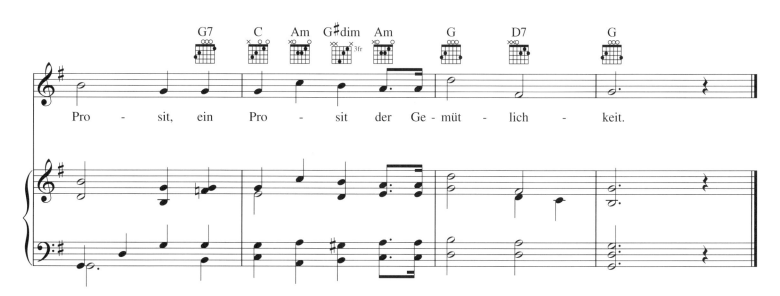

Pro - sit, ein Pro - sit der Ge - müt - lich - keit.

# DOWN BY THE SALLEY GARDENS

Poem by WILLIAM BUTLER YEATS
Music from Irish Air "The Maids of Mourne Shore"

# DRILL, YE TARRIERS, DRILL

Words and Music by
THOMAS CASEY

# EARLY ONE MORNING

Traditional English Folksong

**Tenderly**

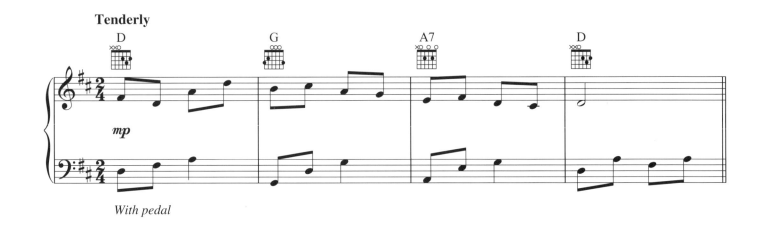

*mp*

*With pedal*

1. Ear - ly one morn - ing just as the sun was
mem - ber the vows _____ that you made _____ to your
3., 4. *(See additional lyrics)*

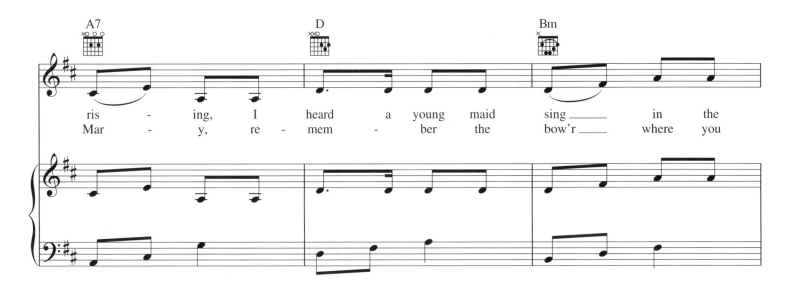

ris - ing, I heard a young maid sing _____ in the
Mar - y, re - mem - ber the bow'r _____ where you

**Chorus**

val - ley be - low:) vowed ___ to be true.) Oh, don't de - ceive ___ me. Oh, nev - er leave ___ me. How ___ could you use ___ a ___ poor ___ maid - en so?

2. Re - so?
3. Oh,
4. Thus

*rit.*

*Additional Lyrics*

3. Oh, gay is the garland and frewsh are the roses
   I've culled from the garden to place upon thy brow.
   *Chorus*

4. Thus sang the poor maiden, her sorrows bewailing,
   Thus sang the poor maid in the valley below:
   *Chorus*

# EVERY NIGHT WHEN THE SUN GOES DOWN

Southern Appalachian Folksong

# EVERY TIME I FEEL THE SPIRIT

African-American Spiritual

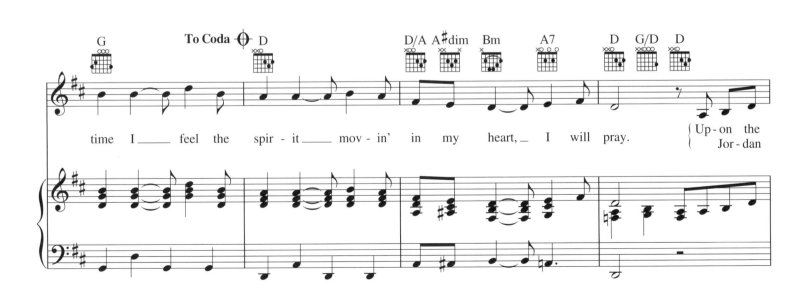

# EZEKIEL SAW THE WHEEL

African-American Spiritual

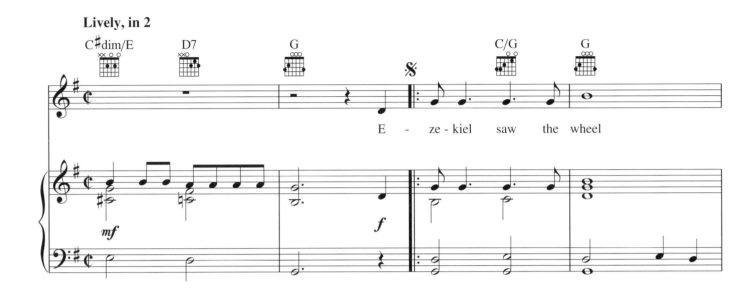

E - ze - kiel saw the wheel 'way up in the mid - dle of the air. E - ze - kiel saw the wheel

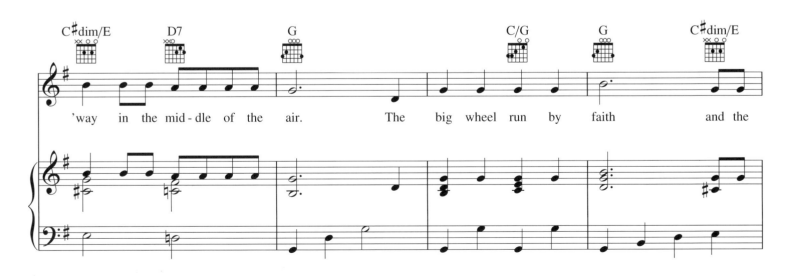

'way in the mid - dle of the air. The big wheel run by faith and the

# FLOW GENTLY, SWEET AFTON

Words by ROBERT BURNS
Music by ALEXANDER HUME

# FOLLOW THE DRINKIN' GOURD

African-American Spiritual

# FRÈRE JACQUES
## (Are You Sleeping?)

French Folksong

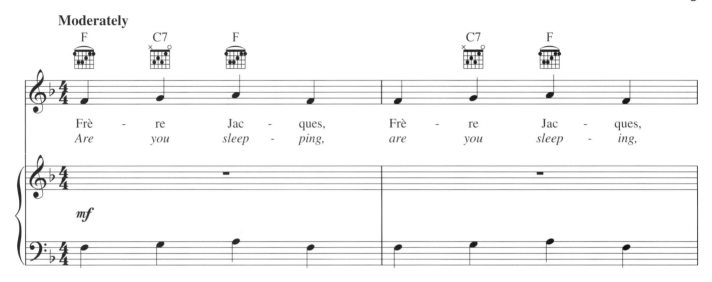

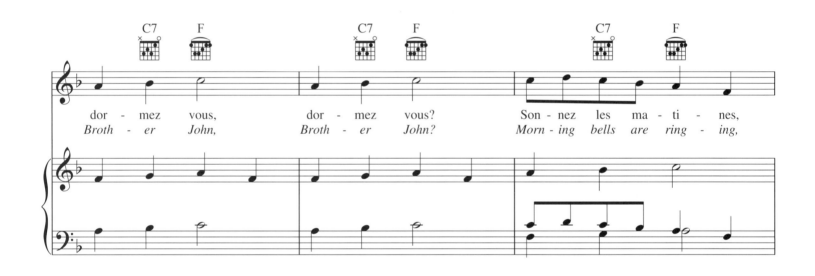

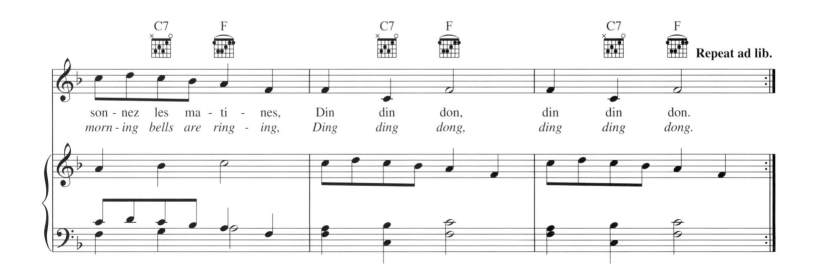

# GAUDEAMUS IGITUR

Words by C.W. KINDLEBEN, 1781
Traditional Melody

**Additional Lyrics**

4. Vivat academia,
   Vivant professores!
   Vivat membrum quodlibet,
   Vivat membra quælibet,
   Semper sint in flore!

5. Vivant omnes virgines,
   Faciles, formosæ!
   Vivant et mulieres,
   Teneræ, amabiles,
   Bonæ laboriosæ!

6. Vivat et republica
   Et qui illam regit!
   Vivat nostra civitas,
   Mæcenatum caritas,
   Quæ nos hic protegit!

7. Pereat tristitia,
   Pereant osores,
   Pereat diabolus,
   Quivis antiburschius
   Atque irrisores!

# FUNICULI, FUNICULA

Words and Music by
LUIGI DENZA

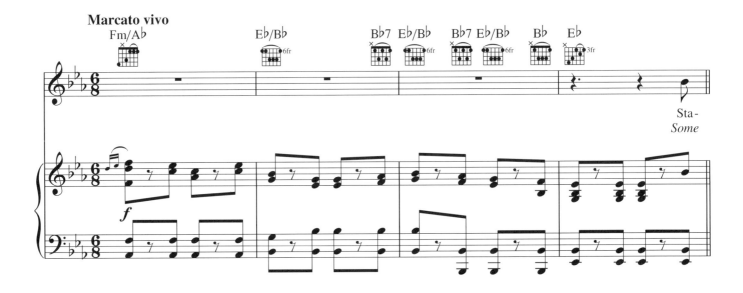

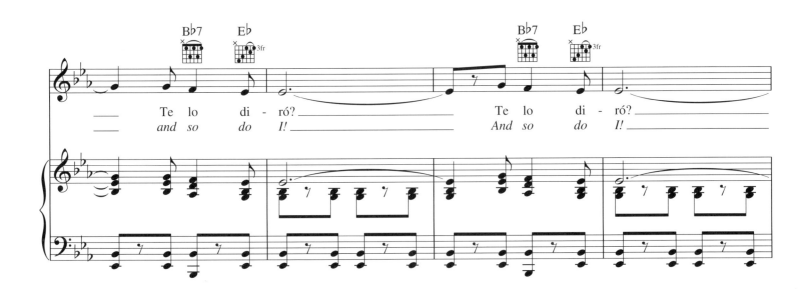

# THE GALWAY PIPER

Irish Folksong

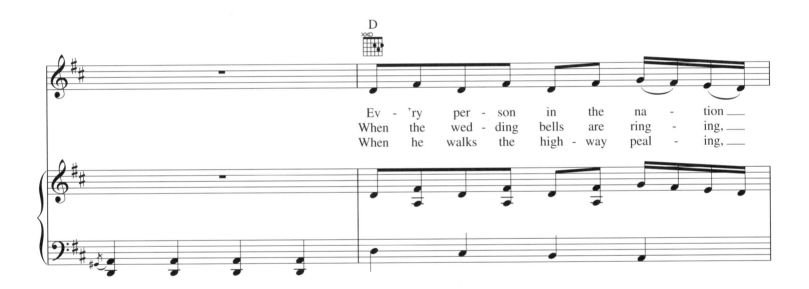

# GET ALONG, LITTLE DOGIES

Traditional American Cowboy Song

# GO DOWN, MOSES

African-American Spiritual

# GOODBYE, OLD PAINT

Western American Cowboy Song

# GREAT DAY

African-American Spiritual

# THE GOSPEL TRAIN

African-American Spiritual

# HATIKVAH
## (With Hope)

Words by N.H. IMBER
Traditional Hebrew Melody

# HE'S GONE AWAY

American Folksong

# HIGH BARBAREE

American Sea Chantey
sometimes attributed to CHARLES DIBDIN

1. There were two loft - y ships from old Eng - land ___
(2.) loft ___ there, a - loft! our ___ jol - ly boat - swain
(3.) naught up - on the stern, there's ___ naught up - on the
(4.) hail ___ her! O hail her!" our gal - lant cap - tain
(5.) I am not a man - o'- war or a pri - va - teer," said
6., 7. *(See additional lyrics)*

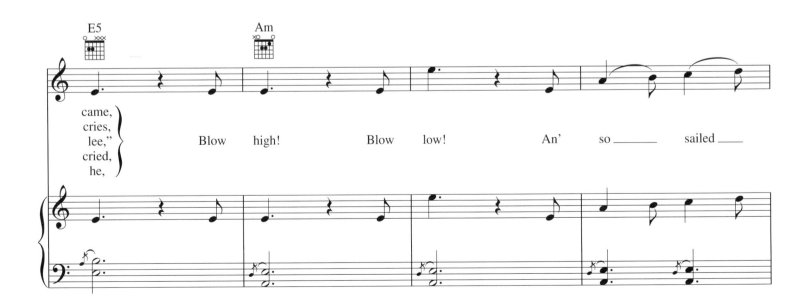

came,
cries,
lee,"
cried,
he,

Blow high! Blow low! An' so ___ sailed ___

*Additional Lyrics*

6. Oh, 'twas broadside to broadside a long time we lay,
Blow high! Blow low! An' so sailed we.
Until the Prince of Luther show the pirate's masts away.
All a-cruisin' down the coasts of the High Barbaree!

7. "O quarter! O quarter!" those pirates then did cry,
Blow high! Blow low! An' so sailed we.
But the quarter that we gave them—we sunk them in the sea.
All a-cruisin' down the coasts of the High Barbaree!

# HOW CAN I KEEP FROM SINGING

Words and Music by
REV. ROBERT LOWREY

# THE HURON CAROL

Words by JESSE EDGAR MIDDLETON
16th Century French Melody

**Moderately, with a steady beat**

1. 'Twas in the moon of win-ter-time, when
   in a lodge of bro-ken bark the
3., 4. *(See additional lyrics)*

all the birds had fled, that might-y Git-chi Man-i-tou sent
ten-der Babe was found. A rag-ged robe of rab-bit skin en-

an-gel choirs in-stead. Be-fore the light the stars grew dim, and
wrapped His beau-ty 'round. And as the hunt-er braves drew nigh, the

*Additional Lyrics*

3. The earliest moon of wintertime is not so round and fair
   As was the ring of glory or the helpless Infant there.
   The chiefs from far before Him knelt
   With gifts of fur and beaver pelt.
   Jesus, your king, is born.
   Jesus is born,
   In excelsis gloria!

4. O children of the forest free, O sons of Manitou,
   The Holy Child of earth and heav'n is born today for you.
   Come kneel before the radiant Boy
   Who brings you beauty, peace, and joy.
   Jesus, your king, is born.
   Jesus is born,
   In excelsis gloria!

# I GOT A ROBE

African-American Spiritual

# I KNOW WHERE I'M GOIN'

English Folksong

Gently

I know where I'm go - ing, and
I'll wear stock-ings of silk, and
Feath - er beds are soft, and
Some say he's poor, but

I know who's go - ing with me.
shoes of bright green leath - er,
paint - ed rooms are bon - nie,
I say he's bon - nie,

I know who I love, but the
combs to buck-le my hair, and a
but I would trade them all for my
fair - est of them all is my

Lord knows who I'll mar - ry.
ring for ev - 'ry fin - ger.
hand - some, win - some John - ny.
hand - some, win - some

John - ny.

# JOHN HENRY

West Virginia Folksong

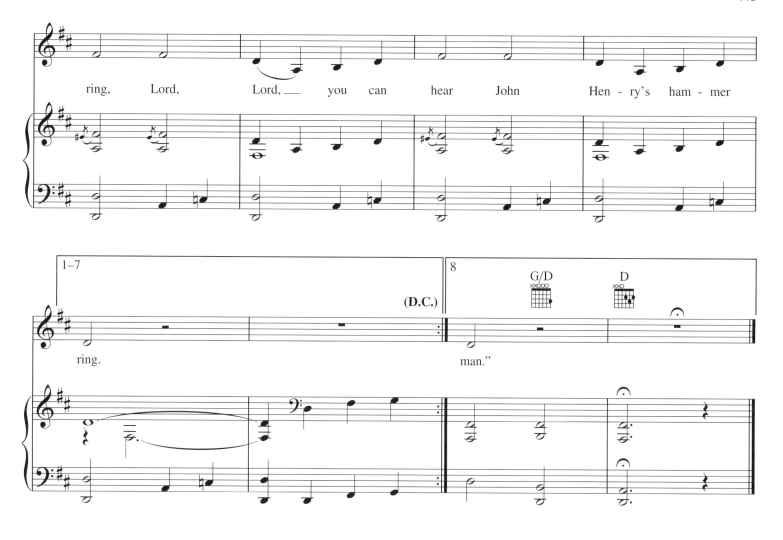

ring,    Lord,    Lord, ____ you can hear John    Hen - ry's ham - mer

ring.

man."

**Additional Lyrics**

2. When John Henry was a little boy,
   A-sitting on his papa's knee,
   He picked up a hammer and a little
      piece of steel,
   Said, "Hammer's gonna be the death
      of me"...

3. Well, the captain said to John Henry,
   "Gonna bring me a steam drill 'round,
   Gonna bring me a steam drill out on the job.
   Gonna whup that steel on down"...

4. John Henry said to his captain,
   "A man ain't nothin' but a man,
   And before I let that steam drill beat
      me down,
   I'll die with a hammer in my hand"...

5. John Henry said to his shaker,
   "Shaker, why don't you pray?
   'Cause if I miss this little piece of steel,
   Tomorrow be your buryin' day"...

6. John Henry was driving on the mountain
   And his hammer was flashing fire.
   And the last words I heard that poor boy say,
   "Gimme a cool drink of water 'fore I die"...

7. John Henry, he drove fifteen feet,
   The steam drill only made nine.
   But he hammered so hard that he broke
      his poor heart,
   And he laid down his hammer and he died...

8. They took John Henry to the graveyard
   And they buried him in the sand.
   And every locomotive comes a-roaring by says,
   "There lies a steel-driving man"...

# I NEVER WILL MARRY

Traditional Folksong

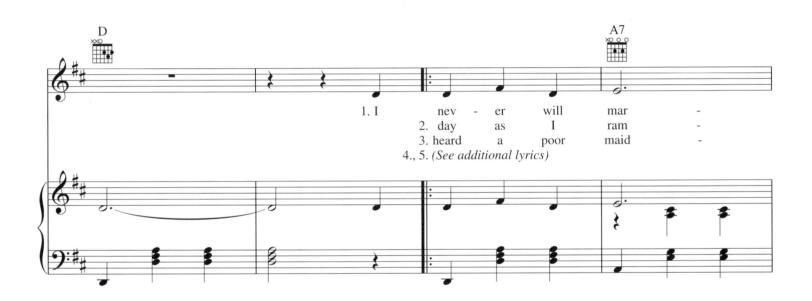

1. I nev - er will mar -
2. day as I ram -
3. heard a poor maid -
4., 5. *(See additional lyrics)*

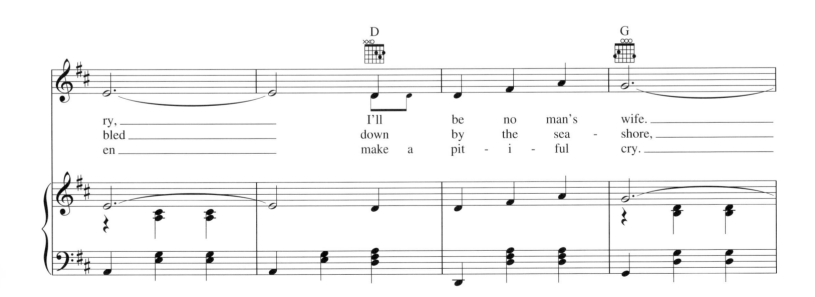

ry, _____ I'll be no man's wife. _____
bled _____ down by the sea - shore, _____
en _____ make a pit - i - ful cry. _____

*Additional Lyrics*

4. "My love's gone and left me, he's the one I adore.
   I never will see him, no never, no more."

5. "The shells in the ocean will be my deathbed,
   And the fish in the water swim over my head."

6. She plunged her fair body in the water so deep.
   And she closed her pretty blue eyes in the water to sleep.

# I'S THE B'Y

Newfoundland Folksong

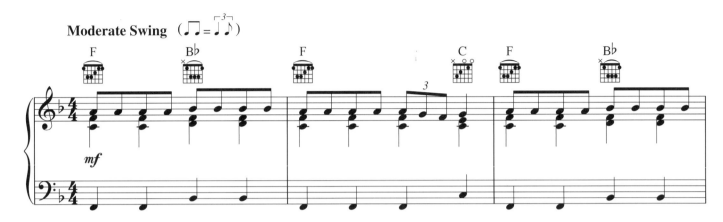

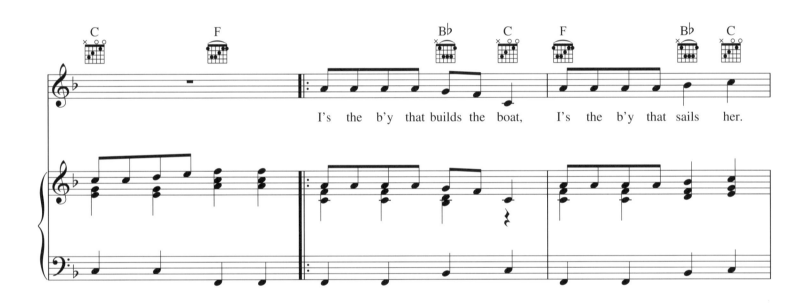

I's the b'y that builds the boat, I's the b'y that sails her.

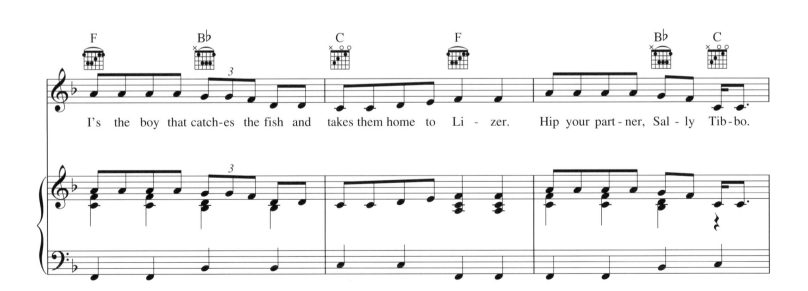

I's the boy that catch-es the fish and takes them home to Li - zer. Hip your part - ner, Sal - ly Tib-bo.

# I'VE GOT PEACE LIKE A RIVER

Traditional

# JENNY JENKINS

18th Century American Folksong

1. Will you wear white, oh my dear, oh my dear? Oh, will you wear
2. Will you wear green, oh my dear, oh my dear? Oh, will you wear
3. Will you wear blue, oh my dear, oh my dear? Oh, will you wear
4.–6. *(See additional lyrics)*

white, Jen - ny Jen - kins? _____ No, I won't wear white, for the
green, Jen - ny Jen - kins? _____ No, I won't wear green, it's the
blue, Jen - ny Jen - kins? _____ No, I won't wear blue, for the

**Chorus**

*Additional Lyrics*

4. Will you wear yellow, oh my dear, oh my dear?
   Oh, will you wear yellow, Jenny Jenkins?
   No, I won't wear yellow, for I'd never get a fellow.
   *Chorus*

5. Will you wear brown, oh my dear, oh my dear?
   Oh, will you wear brown, Jenny Jenkins?
   No, I won't wear brown, for I'd never get around.
   *Chorus*

6. Will you wear beige, oh my dear, oh my dear?
   Oh, will you wear beige, Jenny Jenkins?
   No, I won't wear beige, for it shows my age.
   *Chorus*

# JESSE JAMES

Missouri Folksong

# JOHNNY HAS GONE FOR A SOLDIER

American Revolutionary War Song
Based on a 17th Century Irish Tune

# LA MARSEILLAISE

Words and Music by
CLAUDE ROUGET DE LISLE

## Additional Lyrics

2. Amour Sacré de la Patrie,
   Conduis, soutiens, nos bras vengeurs.
   Liberté, liberté chérie
   Combats avec tes défenseurs!
   Combats avec tes défenseurs!
   Sous nos drapeaux, que la victoire
   Accours à tes mâles accents!
   Que tes ennemis expirants
   Voient ton triomphe et notre gloire.
      Aux armes, etc.

3. Nous enterons dans la carrière
   Quand nos aînés n'y seront plus.
   Nous y trouverons leur poussière
   Et la trace de leurs vertus,
   Et la trace de leurs vertus,
   Bien moins jaloux de leur survivre
   Que de partager leur cercueil
   Nous aurons le sublime orgueil
   De les venger ou de les suivre.
      Aux armes, etc.

## English Translation

1. *Arise you children of our Motherland,*
   *Oh now is here our glorious day!*
   *Over us the bloodstained banner*
   *Of tyranny holds sway!*
   *Of tyranny holds sway!*
   *Oh, do you hear there in our fields*
   *The roar of those fierce fighting men*
   *Who came right here into our midst*
   *To slaughter sons, wives and kin?*
      *To arms, oh citizens!*
      *Form up in serried ranks!*
      *March on, march on!*
      *And drench our fields*
      *With their tainted blood!*

2. *Supreme devotion to our Motherland,*
   *Guides and sustains avenging hands.*
   *Liberty, oh dearest Liberty,*
   *Come fight with your shielding bands!*
   *Come fight with your shielding bands!*
   *Beneath our banner come, oh Victory,*
   *Run at your soul-stirring cry.*
   *Oh come, come see your foes now die,*
   *Witness your pride and our glory.*
      *To arms, etc.*

3. *Into the fight we too shall enter,*
   *When our fathers are dead and gone,*
   *We shall find their bones laid down to rest*
   *With the fame of their glories won,*
   *With the fame of their glories won!*
   *Oh, to survive them care we not,*
   *Glad are we to share their grave,*
   *Great honor is to be our lot*
   *To follow or to venge our brave.*
      *To arms, etc.*

# THE JOLLY MILLER

English Folksong

# KRAKOWIAK
## (Darling Maiden, Hark, I Ask Thee)

Polish Folksong

# LA VERA SORRENTINA
## (The Fair Maid of Sorrento)

Neapolitan Folksong

tèt - ta _____ no - mi - nà. Da chel - gà!

*Additional Lyrics*

2. Da chell' ora nn'aggio pace,
   Stongo sempe a sosperare;
   Chiù la rezza non me piace,
   Chiù no ntenno lo ppescare.
   Co la misera barchetta
   A Sorriento 'nfretta, 'nfretta
   Ogne sera, ogne mattina
   Vace lagreme a jettà.
   Ma la sgrata Sorrentina
   Non ha maje de me pietà.

3. Se non cura chesti pene
   Quanto cana, tanto bella,
   Voto strada, e do lo bbene
   A quacc' altra nennella,
   Ma che vedo? che sventura,
   Lampa, e l'aria se fa scura.
   Aggio spersa la banchina
   La barchetta è p'affonnà!
   Pe tte sprata Sorrentina
   Io mi vado ad affogà!

# LANDLORD, FILL THE FLOWING BOWL

Traditional

# THE LARK IN THE CLEAR AIR

Words and Music by
SIR SAMUEL FERGUSON

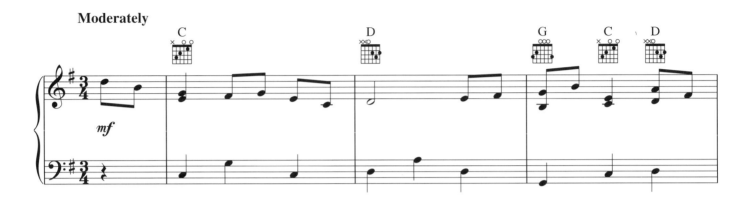

Dear ___ thoughts are ___ in my mind, and ___ my
tell her ___ all my love, and ___ my

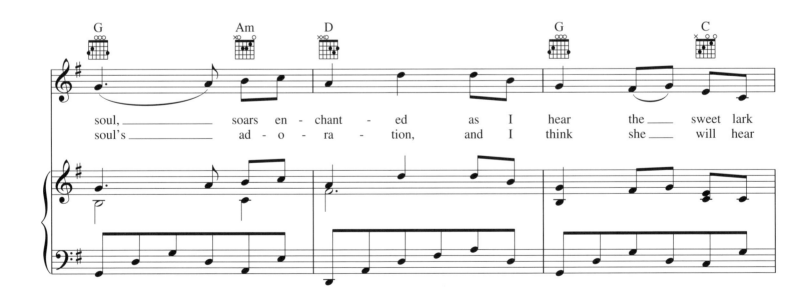

soul, ___ soars en - chant - ed as I hear the ___ sweet lark
soul's ___ ad - o - ra - tion, and I think she ___ will hear

# LET US BREAK BREAD TOGETHER

African-American Spiritual

# LIGHTLY ROW

Traditional

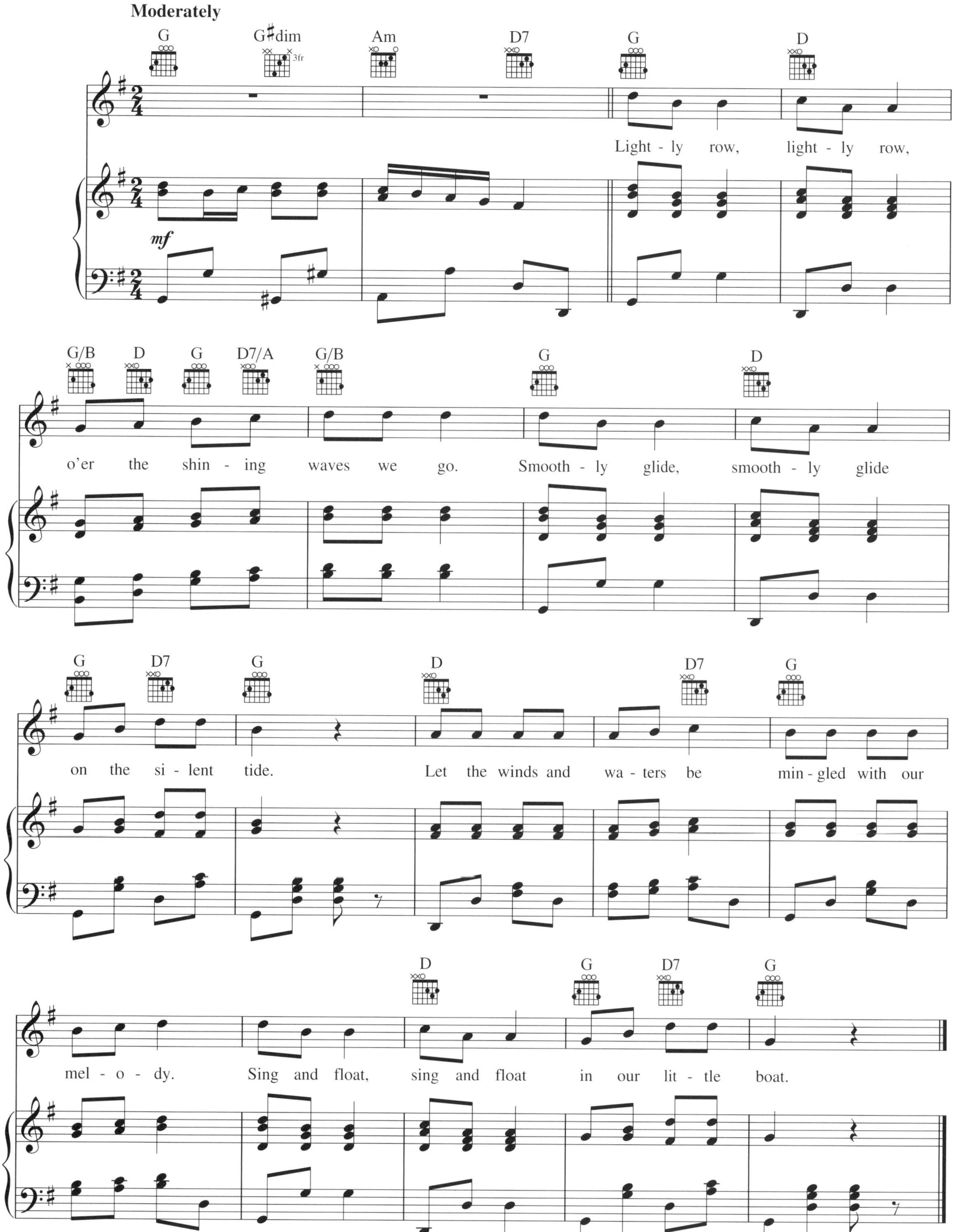

# THE LONESOME ROAD

African-American Spiritual

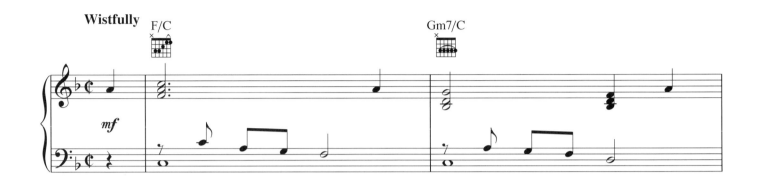

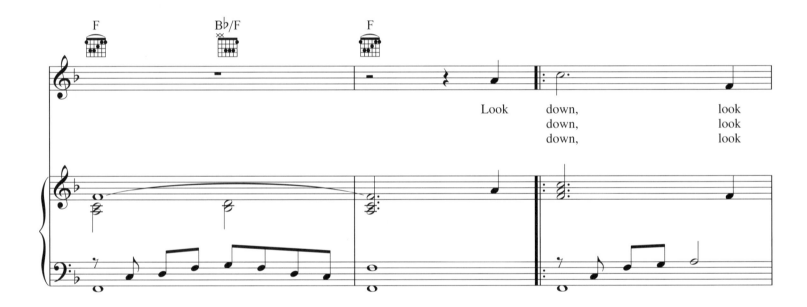

Look  down,  look
down,  look
down,  look

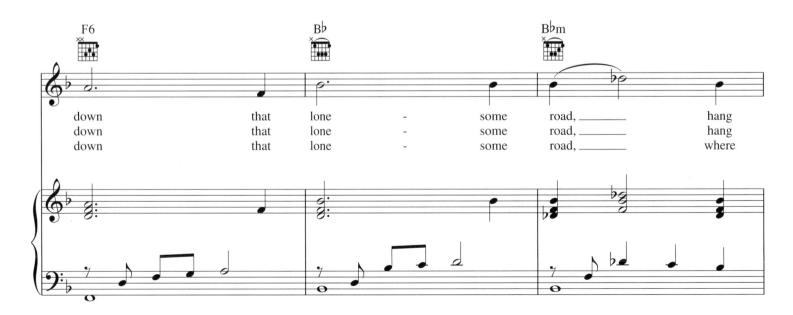

down  that  lone - some  road, _____  hang
down  that  lone - some  road, _____  hang
down  that  lone - some  road, _____  where

# LORD, I WANT TO BE A CHRISTIAN

African-American Spiritual

# LOVE SOMEBODY

Traditional

# MAN OF CONSTANT SORROW

Appalachian Folksong

*Additional Lyrics*

3. I'm a man of constant sorrow.
   Farewell to the one I love.
   I'm bound to take the lonely highway,
   Till the Lord takes me above.

4. I'm a man of constant sorrow,
   A stranger in every town.
   Friends I have none to give me comfort
   While I go roaming 'round.

5. I'm a man of constant sorrow.
   My face you may see no more.
   One thing I know I can be sure of:
   We'll meet on one same shore.

6. I'm a man of constant sorrow.
   I've seen trouble all my days.
   I left my home in old Kentucky,
   Where I was born and raised.

# MARY HAD A BABY

African-American Spiritual

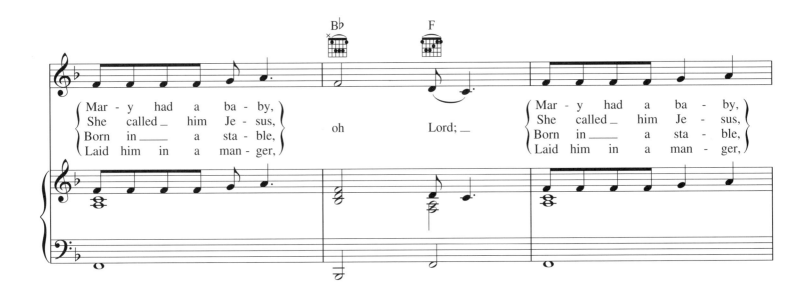

Mary had a ba-by, She called him Je-sus, Born in a sta-ble, Laid him in a man-ger, oh Lord; Mary had a ba-by, She called him Je-sus, Born in a sta-ble, Laid him in a man-ger,

oh my Lord; Mary had a ba-by, She called him Je-sus, Born in a sta-ble, Laid him in a man-ger, oh Lord; the

# MATILDA

Traditional Folksong

**Calypso beat**

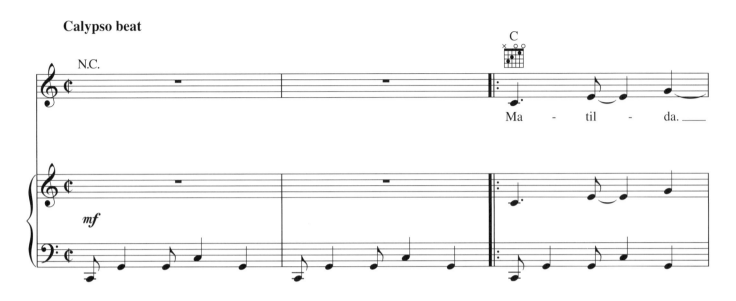

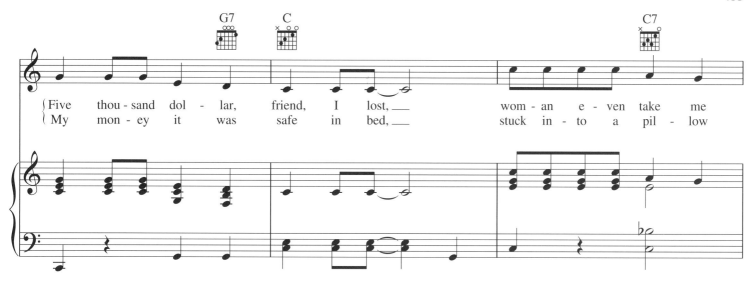

Five thou - sand dol - lar, friend, I lost, ___ wom - an e - ven take me
My mon - ey it was safe in bed, ___ stuck in - to a pil - low

cart and horse. ___ Mon - ey was to buy me house and lot, ___
for me head. ___ Hid - ing from Ma - til - da was in vain, ___

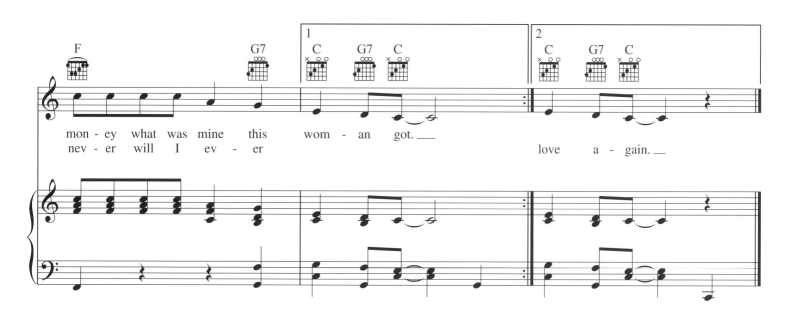

mon - ey what was mine this wom - an got. ___
nev - er will I ev - er love a - gain. ___

# MEIN HUT, DER HAT DREI ECKEN

Words Anonymous
Melody by NICOLÒ PAGANINI

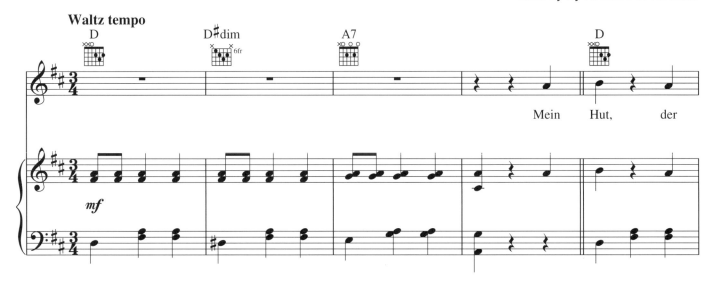

Mein Hut, der

hat drei Ec - ken, drei Ec - ken hat mein

Hut, _____ und hat er nicht ___ drei Ec - ken,

# MEXICAN HAT DANCE
## (Jarabe Topatio)

By F.A. PARTICHELA

**Tempo I**

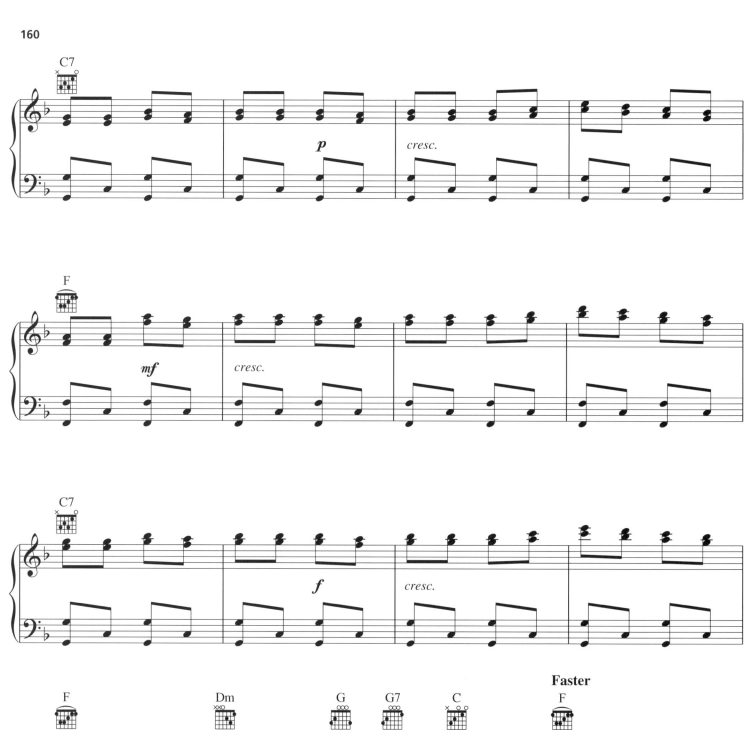

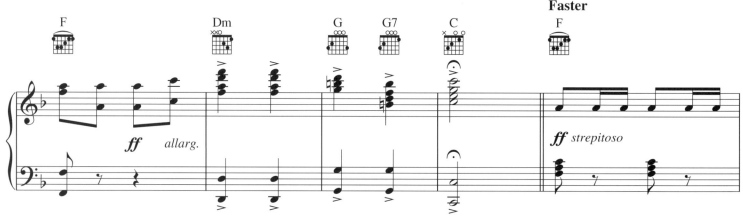

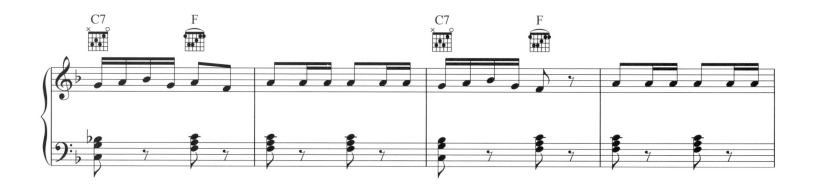

# THE MINSTREL BOY

Words by THOMAS MOORE
Traditional Irish Air, "The Moreen"

# MRS. MURPHY'S CHOWDER

Irish Folksong

Won't you

bring back, won't you bring back Mis - sus Mur - phy's chow - der? It was
bring back, won't you bring back Mis - sus Mur - phy's chow - der? From each
bring back, won't you brink back Mis - sus Mur - phy's chow - der? You can

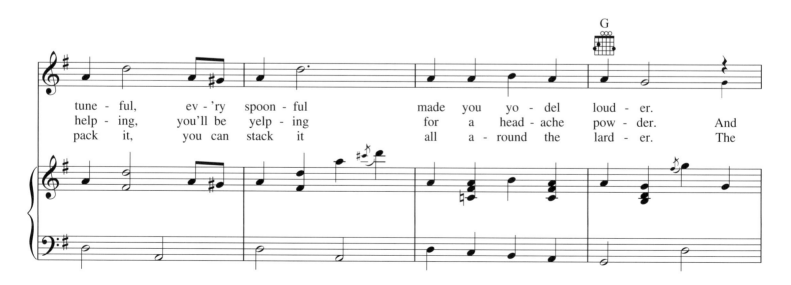

tune - ful, ev - 'ry spoon - ful made you yo - del loud - er.
help - ing, you'll be yelp - ing for a head - ache pow - der. And
pack it, you can stack it all a - round the lard - er. The

8vb

# OLD JOE CLARK

Tennessee Folksong

**Square Dance tempo**

1. Old Joe Clark, the preach-er's son, preached all o-ver the plain; the
3., 5. *(See additional lyrics)*

on - ly text he ev - er used was high low jack and the game.

**Chorus**

Round and a-round, Old Joe Clark, round and a-round, I say; he'd

*Additional Lyrics*

3. When I was a little girl,
   I used to play with toys;
   Now I am a bigger girl,
   I'd rather play with boys.
   *Chorus*

4. When I was a little boy,
   I used to want a knife;
   Now I am a bigger boy,
   I only want a wife.
   *Chorus*

5. Wish I was a sugar tree,
   Standin' in the middle of some town;
   Ev'ry time a pretty girl passed,
   I'd shake some sugar down.
   *Chorus*

6. Old Joe had a yellow cat,
   She would not sing or pray;
   She stuck her head in a buttermilk jar
   And washed her sins away.
   *Chorus*

7. I wish I had a sweetheart;
   I'd set her on the shelf,
   And ev'ry time she'd smile at me
   I'd get up there myself.
   *Chorus*

# NEVER SAID A MUMBLIN' WORD

African-American Spiritual

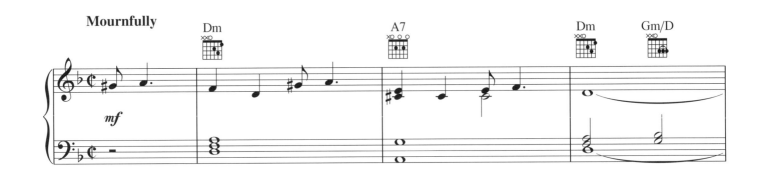

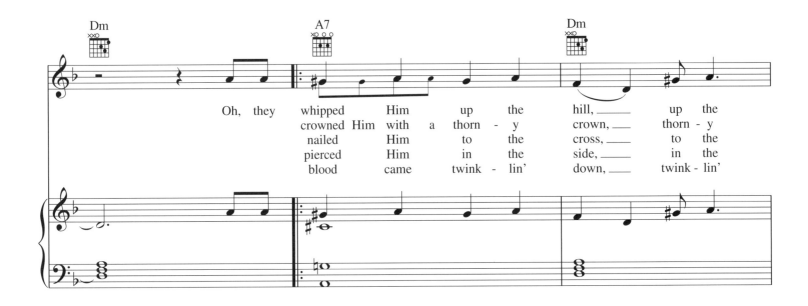

Oh, they whipped Him up the hill, ___ up the
crowned Him with a thorn - y crown, ___ thorn - y
nailed Him to the cross, ___ to the
pierced Him in the side, ___ in the
blood came twink - lin' down, ___ twink - lin'

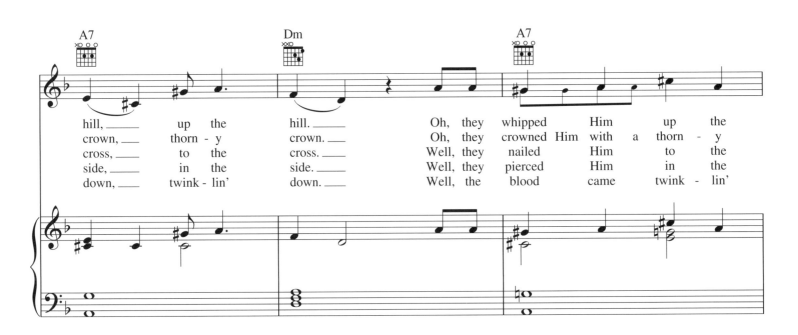

hill, ___ up the hill. ___
crown, ___ thorn - y crown. ___
cross, ___ to the cross. ___
side, ___ in the side. ___
down, ___ twink - lin' down. ___

Oh, they whipped Him up the
Oh, they crowned Him with a thorn - y
Well, they nailed Him to the
Well, they pierced Him in the
Well, the blood came twink - lin'

# O HAPPY DAY

Words by PHILIP DODDRIDGE
Music by EDWARD F. RIMBAULT

# 'O SOLE MIO

Words by GIOVANNI CAPURRO
Music by EDUARDO DI CAPUA

# O TANNENBAUM

Words by HEINRICH ZARNACK (v.1)
and ERNST ANSCHÜTZ (v. 2, 3)
18th Century German Melody

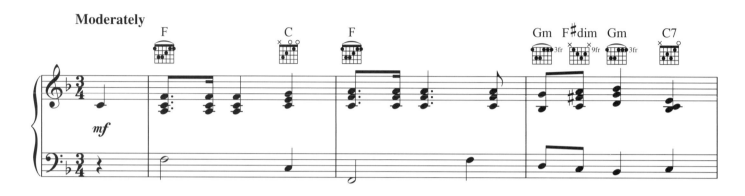

O
Tan - nen - baum, O Tan - nen - baum, wie
Tan - nen - baum, O Tan - nen - baum, du
Tan - nen - baum, O Tan - nen - baum, dein

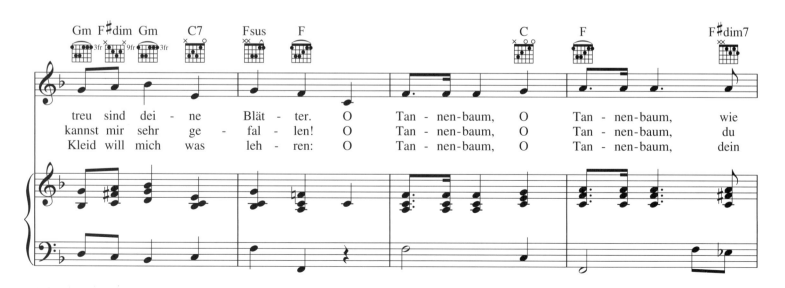

treu sind dei - ne Blät - ter. O Tan - nen - baum, O Tan - nen - baum, wie
kannst mir sehr ge - fal - len! O Tan - nen - baum, O Tan - nen - baum, du
Kleid will mich was leh - ren: O Tan - nen - baum, O Tan - nen - baum, dein

# OH FREEDOM

African-American Spiritual

# ONCE I HAD A SWEETHEART

Southern Appalachian Folksong

# OVER THE WAVES

By JUVENTINO ROSAS

**Waltz tempo**

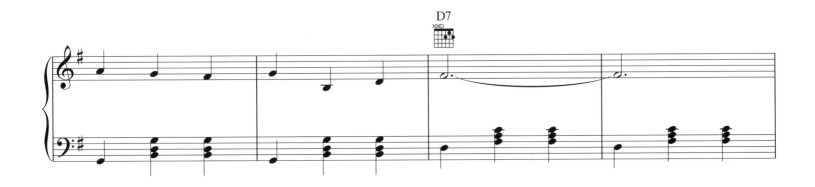

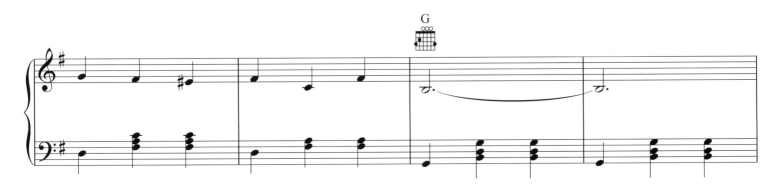

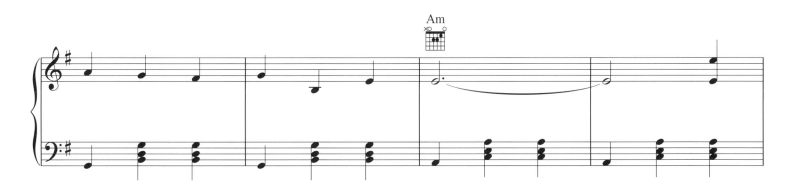

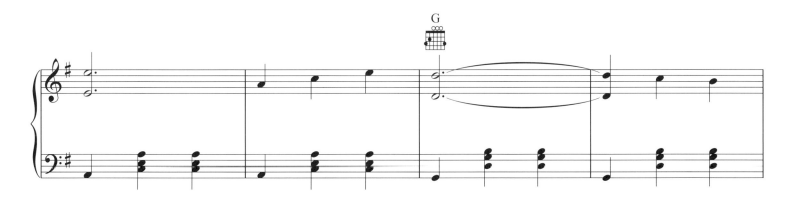

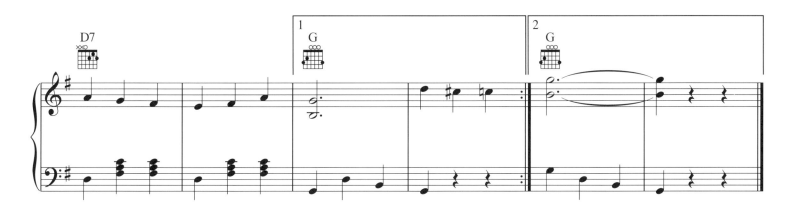

# POP GOES THE WEASEL

Traditional

Lyrics: All a - round the cob - bler's bench the mon - key chased the

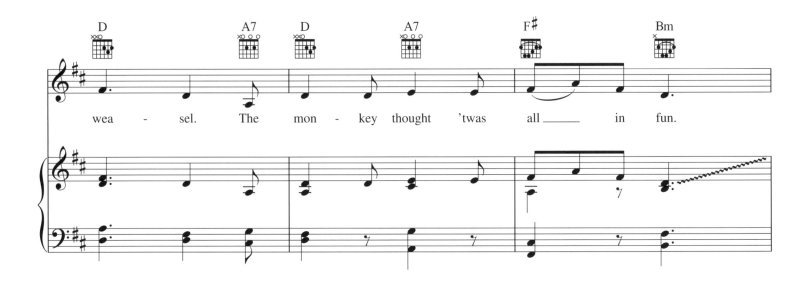

Lyrics: wea - sel. The mon - key thought 'twas all _____ in fun.

Lyrics: Pop! goes the wea - sel. { A pen - y for a spool _ of thread, a / I've

# RAISINS AND ALMONDS
## (Rozhinkes mit mandlen)

By ABRAHAM GOLDFADEN

# THE RED RIVER VALLEY

Traditional American Cowboy Song

From this val - ley they say you are go - ing, _____ you are chang - ing your range for a
sit here a while ere you leave us, _____ do not has - ten to bid us a -

while.    So you say you are wea - ry and ti - red; _____ we shall
dieu.    Come back soon to the Red Riv - er Val - ley, _____ and the

miss your dear face and your smile.    Then come
cow - boy who loves you so    true.

# THE RAMBLING SAILOR

English Sea Chantey

# RING AROUND THE ROSIE

Traditional

**Brightly**

Ring a-round the ros - ie, a pock - et full of po - sies;

ash - es, ash - es, we all fall down.

Lit - tle Sal - ly Wa - ters, sit - ting in a sau - cer,

# ROCK-A-BYE, BABY

Traditional

Rock - a - bye, ba - by, on the tree top, when the wind blows, the cra - dle will rock. When the bough breaks, the cra - dle will fall, and down will come ba - by, cra - dle and all.

# RUE

English Folksong

# SAKURA
## (Cherry Blossoms)

Japanese Folksong

**Gently**

Sa - ku - ra! Sa - ku - ra!
*Sa - ku - ra! Sa - ku - ra!*

*mp*

*With pedal*

Ya yo - i no so ra __ wa, Mi wa - ta - su ka - gi - ri
*Cher - ry blos - soms fill the __ air, smell their fra - grance ev - 'ry - where.*

Ka - su - mi ka ku - mo - ka, Ni o - i - zo i - zu - ru.
*Win - ter - time is fi - n'lly __ past, now the spring is here at __ last.*

I - za - ya! I - za - ya! Mi _____ ni _____ yu - kan.
*Come with me! Come with me! Let us feel the sun - shine fair.*

*rit.*

# SCHNITZELBANK

German Folksong

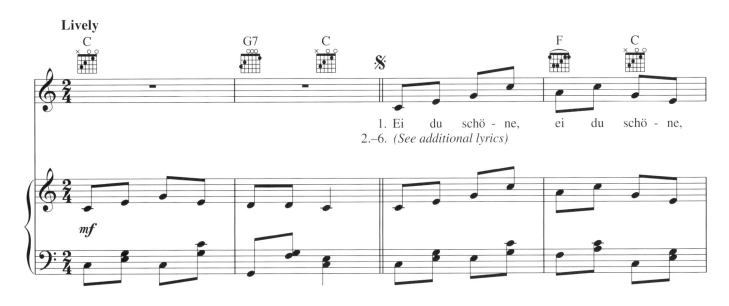

1. Ei du schö - ne, ei du schö - ne,
2.–6. *(See additional lyrics)*

ei du schö - ne Schnit - zel - bank. Ist das nicht ei - ne Schnit - zel - bank?

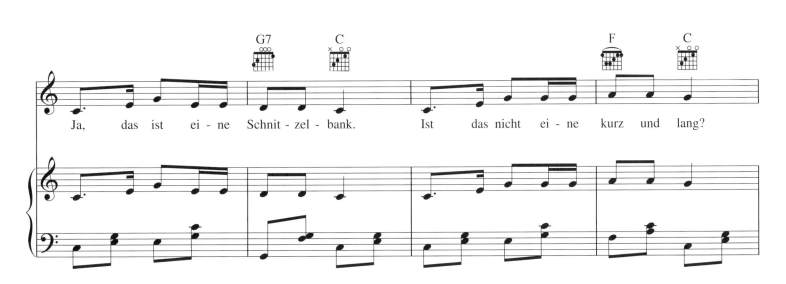

Ja, das ist ei - ne Schnit - zel - bank. Ist das nicht ei - ne kurz und lang?

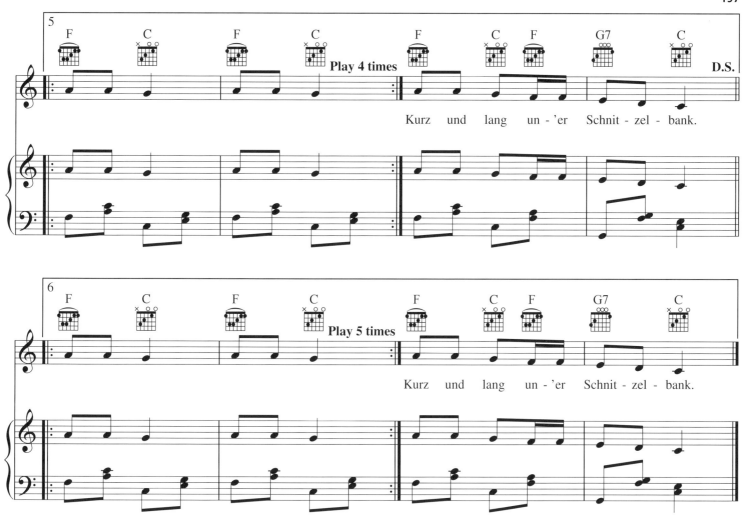

*Additional Lyrics*

2. Ei du schöne, ei du schöne,
   Ei du schöne Schnitzelbank.
   Ist das nicht ein Hin und Her?
   Ja, das ist ein Hin und Her.
   Ist das nicht eine Lichtputzschere?
   Ja, das ist eine Lichtputzschere.
   Lichtputzschere, Hin und Her,
   Kurz und lang un'er Schnitzelbank.

3. Ei du schöne, ei du schöne,
   Ei du schöne Schnitzelbank.
   Ist das nicht ein gold'ner Ring?
   Ja, das ist ein gold'ner Ring.
   Ist das nicht ein schönes Ding?
   Ja, das ist ein schönes Ding.
   Schönes Ding, gold'ner Ring, Lichtputzschere,
   Hin und Her, Kurz und lang un'er Schnitzelbank.

4. Ei du schöne, ei du schöne,
   Ei du schöne Schnitzelbank.
   Ist das nicht ein Krum und Grad?
   Ja, das ist ein Krum und Grad.
   Ist das nicht ein Wagenrad?
   Ja, das ist ein Wagenrad.
   Wagenrad, Krum und Grad,
   Schönes Ding, gold'ner Ring,
   Lichtputzschere, Hin und Her,
   Kurz und lang un'er Schnitzelbank.

5. Ei du schöne, ei du schöne,
   Ei du schöne Schnitzelbank.
   Ist das nicht ein Geisenbock?
   Ja, das ist ein Geisenbock.
   Ist das nicht ein Reifenrock?
   Ja, das ist ein Reifenrock.
   Reifenrock, Geisenbock, Wagenrad,
   Krum und Grad, Schönes Ding,
   Gold'ner Ring, Lichtputzschere, Hin und Her,
   Kurz und lang un'er Schnitzelbank.

6. Ei du schöne, ei du schöne,
   Ei du schöne Schnitzelbank.
   Ist das nicht eine gute Wurst?
   Ja, das ist eine gute Wurst.
   Ist das nicht ein großer Durst?
   Ja, das ist ein großer Durst.
   Großer Durst, gute Wurst,
   Reifenrock, Geisenbock, Wagenrad,
   Krum und Grad, Schönes Ding,
   Gold'ner Ring, Lichtputzschere, Hin und Her,
   Kurz und lang un'er Schnitzelbank.

# SHALOM, CHAVERIM
## (Shalom, Friends)

Traditional Hebrew Round

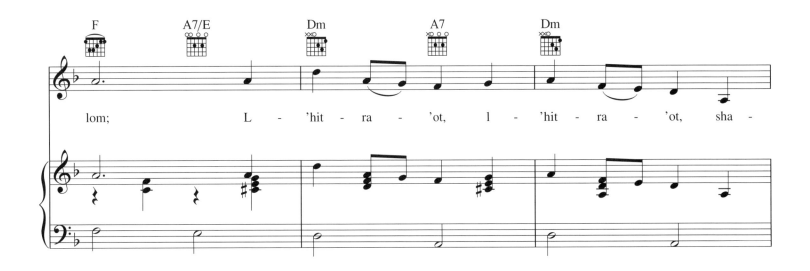

# SHE MOVED THROUGH THE FAIR

Words by PADRAIC COLUM
Traditional Irish Melody

\* kine = money

stepped a - way from me and this she did ___ say: "It ___
then she turned home - ward and with one star a - wake, like a ___
smiled as she passed with her goods and her ___ gear, and ___
laid her hand on me and this she did ___ say: "It ___

will not be long, love, till ___ our wed - ding day."
swan in the eve - ning moves ___ o - ver the lake.
that was the last that I ___ saw of my dear.
will not be long, love, till ___ our wed - ding

*dim.*  ***p***

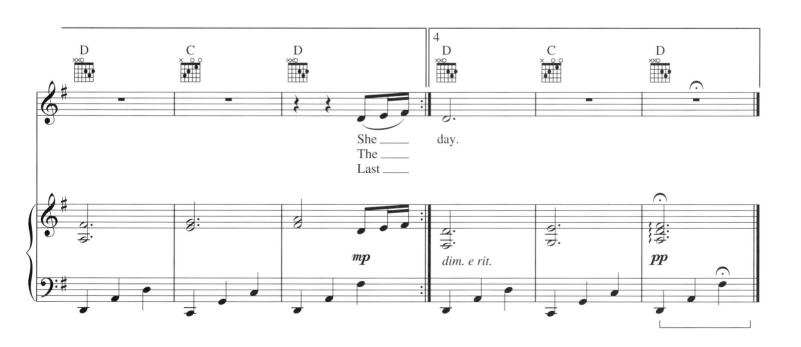

She ___ day.
The ___
Last ___

***mp***    *dim. e rit.*    ***pp***

# SHOO FLY, DON'T BOTHER ME

Words by BILLY REEVES
Music by FRANK CAMPBELL

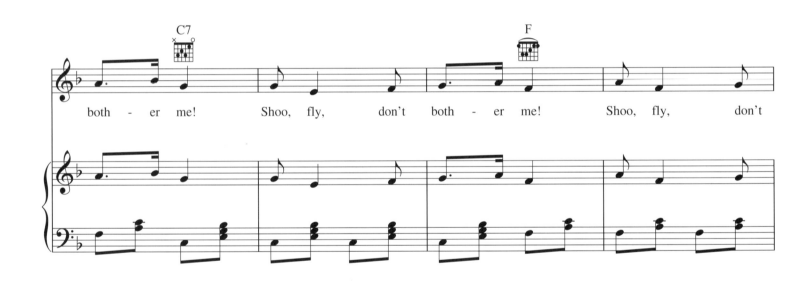

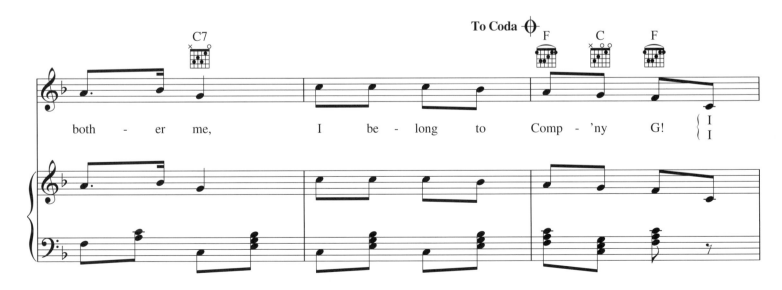

# SIMPLE GIFTS

Traditional Shaker Hymn

# SIYAHAMBA
## (We Are Marching in the Light of God)

South African Traditional

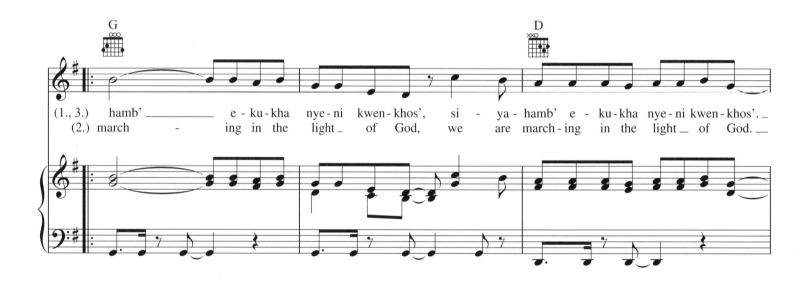

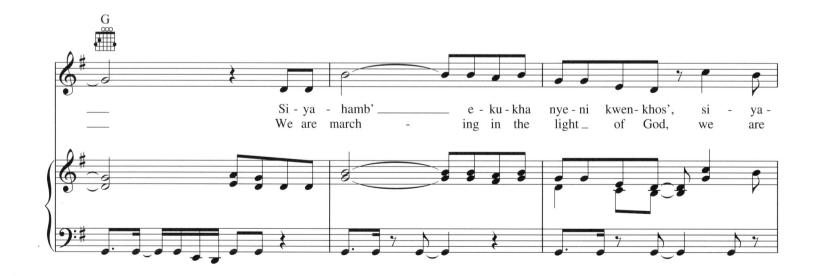

*Pronunciation Guide*

Siyahamba = see-yah-hahm-bah
Ekukha = eh-koo-kah
Nyeni = n_yeh-nee
Kwenkhos' = kwen-k s

# SO LEBEN WIR
## (Long Live the Man)

Words anonymous
"Dessau March," 1706

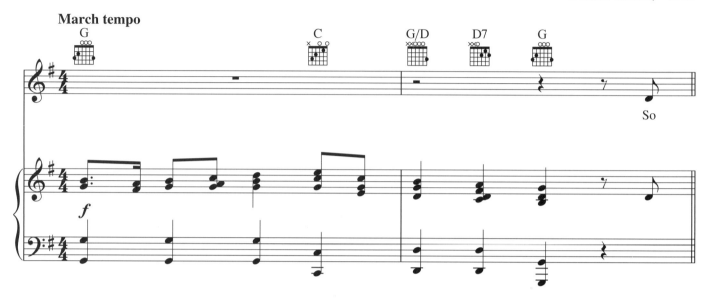

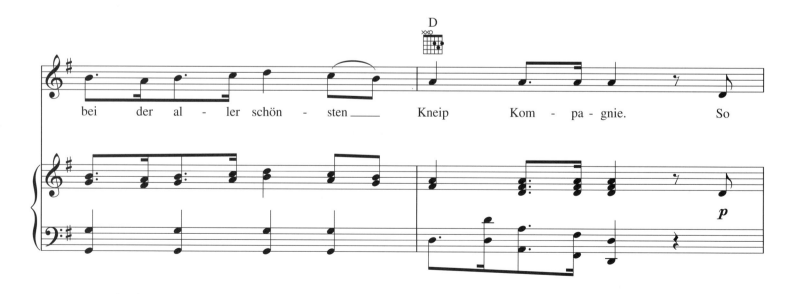

le - ben wir, so le - ben wir, so leb'n wir al - le Ta - ge

bei der al - ler schön - sten ___ Kneip Kom - pa - gnie. Des

Mor - gens bei dem kla - ren Wein, des Mit - tags bei dem Bier, des

A - bends bei den Mäg - de - lein im Nacht - quar - tier.

# SOLDIER, SOLDIER, WILL YOU MARRY ME?

American Folksong

# SOMEBODY'S KNOCKIN' AT YOUR DOOR

African-American Spiritual

# SONG OF THE VOLGA BOATMAN

Russian Folksong

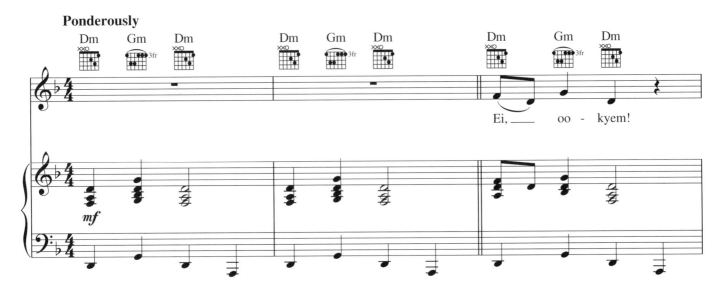

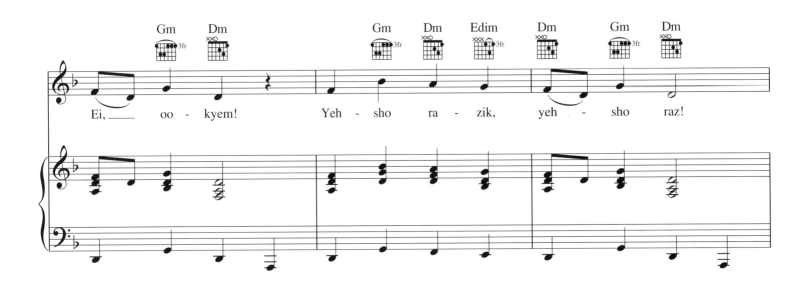

# SOON AH WILL BE DONE

African-American Spiritual

# SOURWOOD MOUNTAIN

Southern Appalachian Folksong

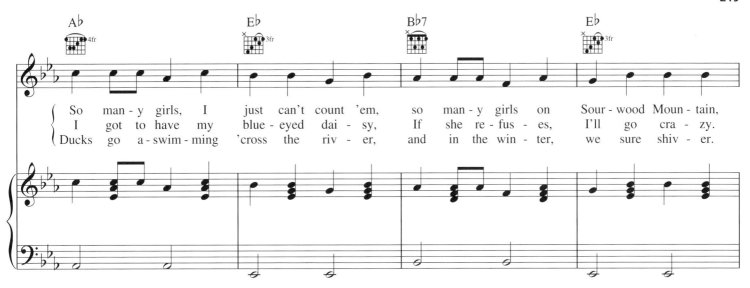

So man-y girls, I just can't count 'em, so man-y girls on Sour-wood Moun-tain,
I got to have my blue-eyed dai-sy, If she re-fus-es, I'll go cra-zy.
Ducks go a-swim-ming 'cross the riv-er, and in the win-ter, we sure shiv-er.

so man-y girls on Sour-wood Moun-tain,
I got to have my blue-eyed dai-sy, } Hey! Hey! Dee-dee um day.
I like __ liv-in' on Sour-wood Moun-tain,

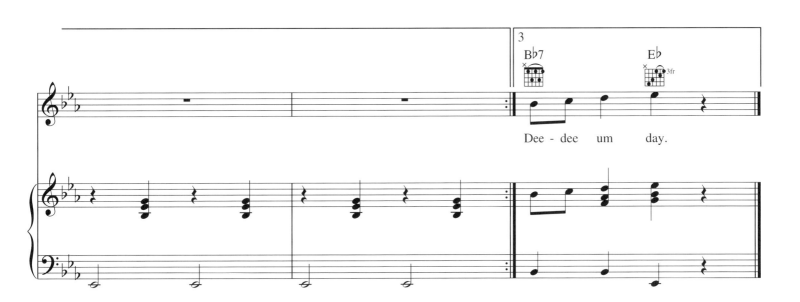

Dee-dee um day.

# STANDIN' IN THE NEED OF PRAYER

African-American Spiritual

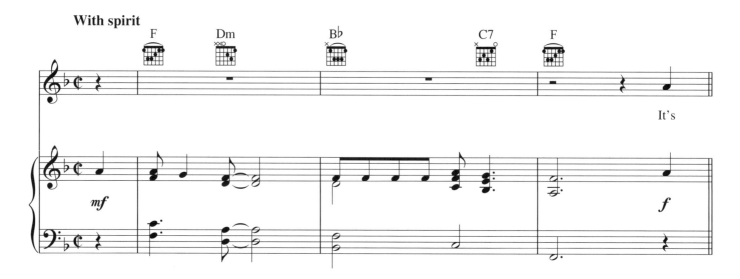

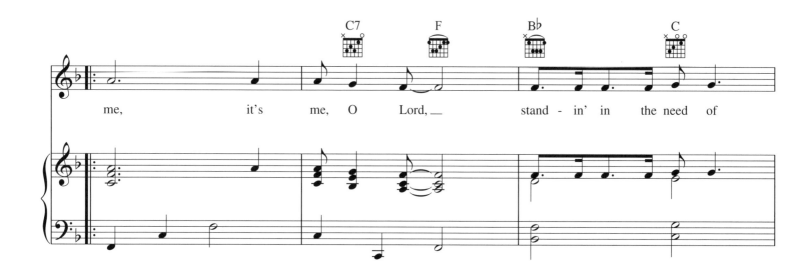

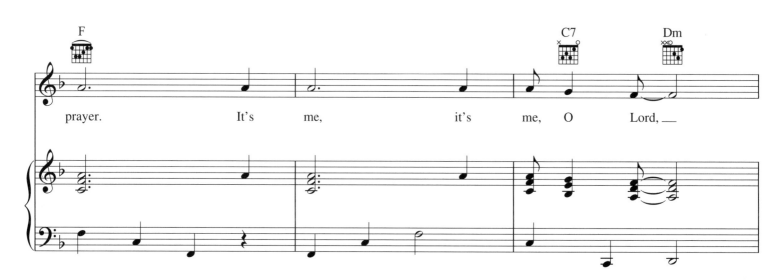

# STAR OF COUNTY DOWN

Irish Folksong

# STEAL AWAY
## (Steal Away to Jesus)

African-American Spiritual

**Moderately**

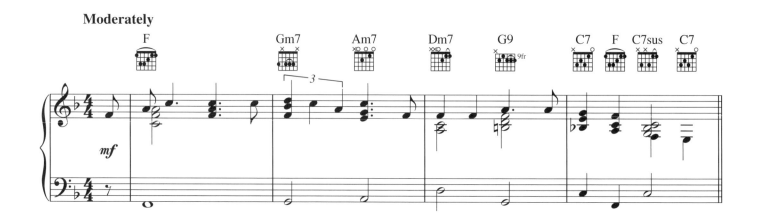

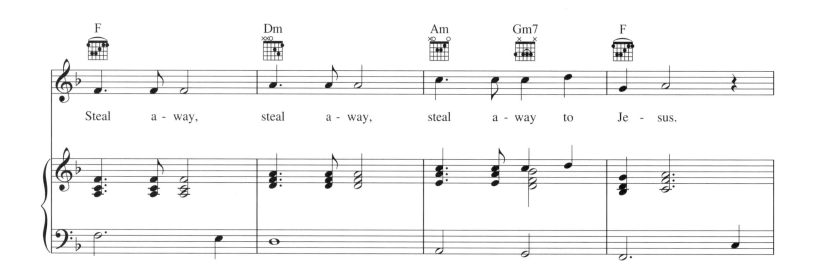

Steal a-way, steal a-way, steal a-way to Je - sus.

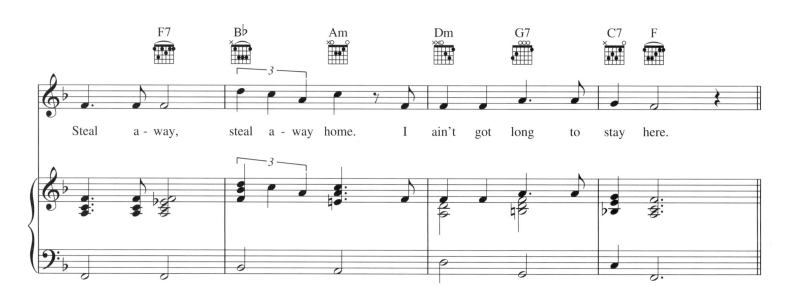

Steal a-way, steal a-way home. I ain't got long to stay here.

# THE STREETS OF LAREDO

American Cowboy Song

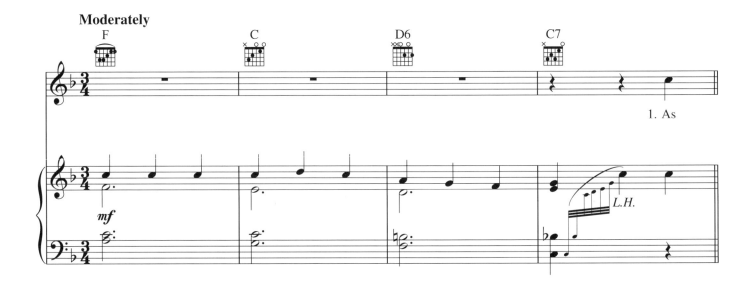

1. As

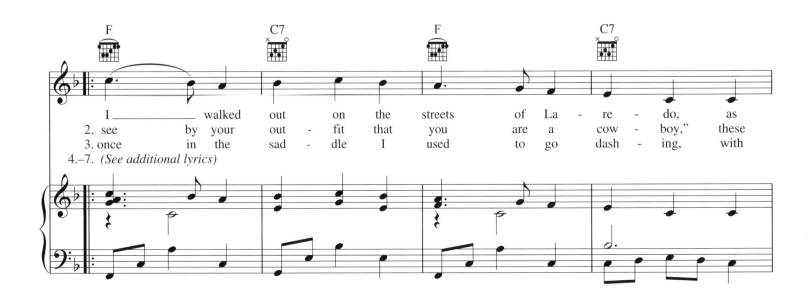

I _____ walked out on the streets of La - re - do, as
2. see by your out - fit that you are a cow - boy," these
3. once in the sad - dle I used to go dash - ing, with
4.–7. *(See additional lyrics)*

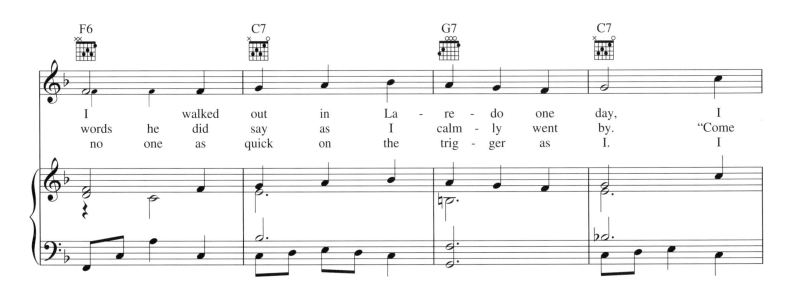

I _____ walked out in La - re - do one day, I
words he did say as I calm - ly went by. "Come
no one as say quick on the trig - ger as I. "I

spied a young cow - boy all wrapped in white lin - en, all
sit down be - side me and hear my sad sto - ry, I'm
sat in a card game in back of the bar - room; got

wrapped in white lin - en and cold as the clay. "I dead.
shot in the breast, and I know I must die." "It was
shot in the back, and to - day I must die." "Get

*Additional Lyrics*

4. "Get six of my buddies to carry my coffin,
   And six pretty maidens to sing a sad song,
   Take me to the valley and lay the sod o'er me,
   For I'm a young cowboy who played the game wrong."

5. "Oh, beat the drum slowly and play the fife lowly,
   And play the dead march as they carry my pall.
   Put bunches of roses all over my coffin,
   The roses will deaden the clods as they fall."

6. "Go gather around you a crowd of young cowboys,
   And tell them the story of this my sad fate.
   Tell one and the other before they go farther,
   To stop their wild roving before it's too late."

7. "Go fetch me a cup, just a cup of cold water,
   To cool my parched lips," the cowboy then said.
   Before I returned, his brave spirit had left him,
   And gone to his Maker, the cowboy was dead.

# THERE IS A BALM IN GILEAD

African-American Spiritual

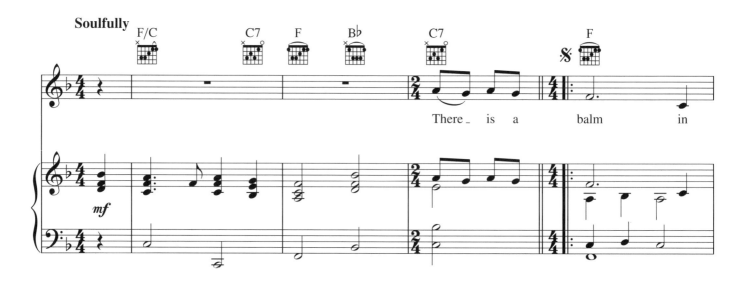

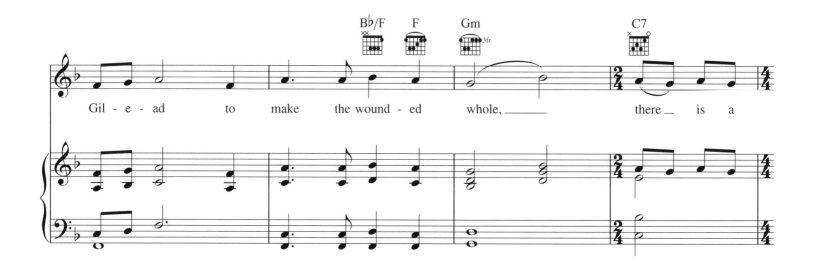

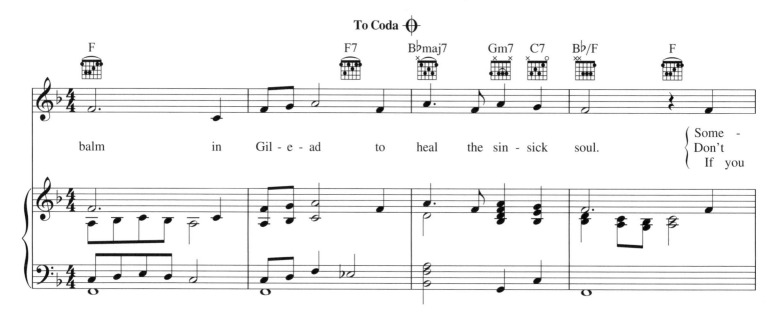

# THERE IS A TAVERN IN THE TOWN

Traditional Drinking Song

There is a tav-ern in the town, in the town, and there my dear love sits him
dig my grave both wide and deep, wide and deep, put tomb-stones at my head and

down, sits him down, and drinks his wine, 'mid laugh-ter free, and
feet, head and feet, and on my breast, carve a tur-tle-dove, to

nev-er, nev-er thinks of me. }
sig-ni-fy I died for love. }

Fare thee well, for I must leave thee, do not

# THREE BLIND MICE

Traditional

Three blind mice, three blind mice! See how they run, see how they run! They all ran af-ter the farm-er's wife; she cut off their tails with a carv-ing knife. Did ev-er you see such a sight in your life as three blind mice?

# VIVE LA COMPAGNIE!

Traditional

# THREE POOR MARINERS

English Folksong

# 'TIS THE LAST ROSE OF SUMMER

Words by THOMAS MOORE
Music by RICHARD ALFRED MILLIKEN

# TOM DOOLEY

Traditional Folksong

# THE WATER IS WIDE
## (O Waly, Waly)

English Folksong

**Moderately slow**

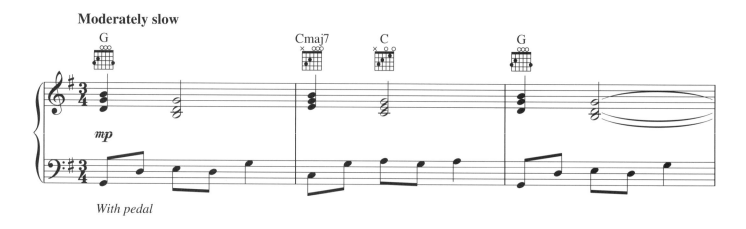

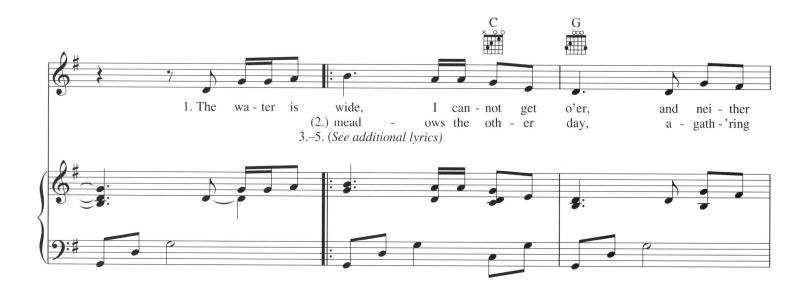

1. The wa-ter is wide, I can-not get o'er, and nei-ther
(2.) mead - ows the oth - er day, a - gath-'ring
3.–5. *(See additional lyrics)*

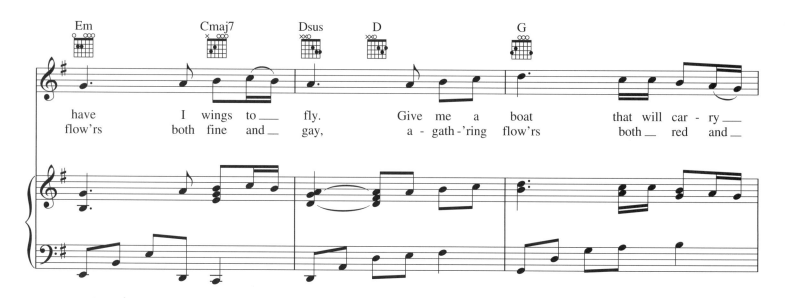

have I wings to ___ fly. Give me a boat that will car-ry ___
flow'rs both fine and ___ gay, a - gath-'ring flow'rs both ___ red and ___

*Additional Lyrics*

3. I leaned my back up against some oak
   Thinking that she was a trusty tree;
   But first she bended and then she broke;
   And so did my false love to me.

4. A ship there is, and she sails the sea,
   She's loaded deep as deep can be,
   But not so deep as the love I'm in:
   I know not if I sink or swim.

5. Oh, love is handsome and love is fine,
   And love's a jew'l while it is new;
   But when it is old, it groweth cold,
   And fades away like morning dew.

# WE ARE CLIMBING JACOB'S LADDER

African-American Spiritual

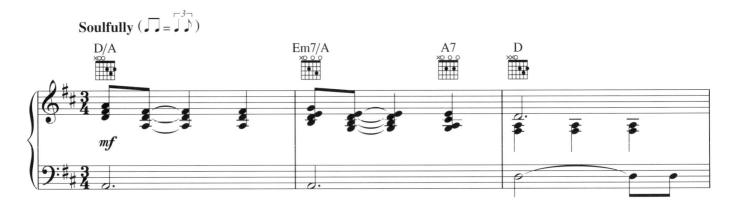

We are ___ climb - ing ___ Ja - cob's ___
Ev - 'ry ___ round goes ___ high - er, ___
We are ___ climb - ing ___ high - er, ___
If you ___ love Him, ___ why not ___

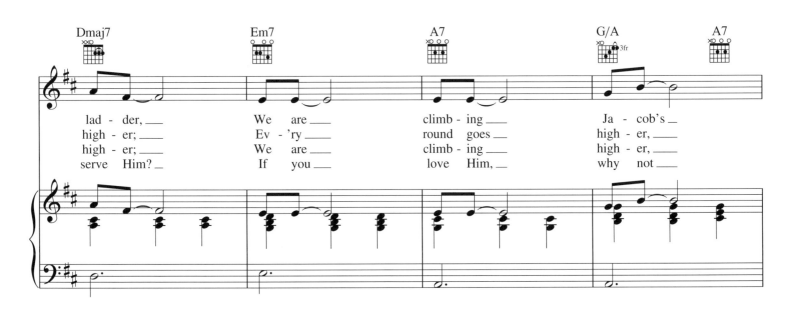

lad - der, ___ We are ___ climb - ing ___ Ja - cob's ___
high - er; ___ Ev - 'ry ___ round goes ___ high - er, ___
high - er; ___ We are ___ climb - ing ___ high - er, ___
serve Him? ___ If you ___ love Him, ___ why not ___

# WERE YOU THERE?

African-American Spiritual

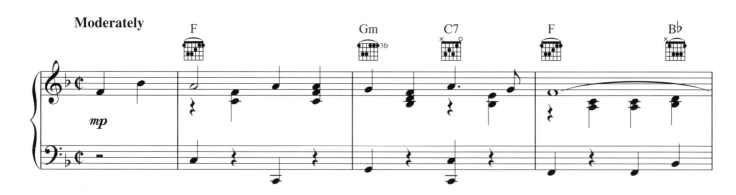

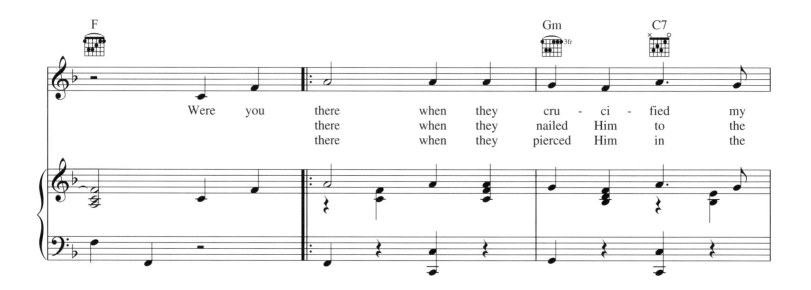

Were you there when they cru - ci - fied my
there when they nailed Him to the
there when they pierced Him in the

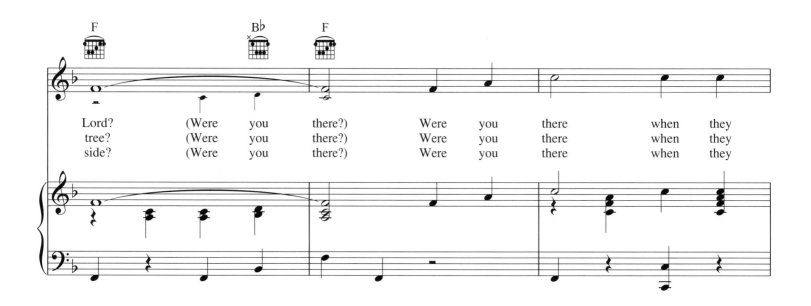

Lord? (Were you there?) Were you there when they
tree? (Were you there?) Were you there when they
side? (Were you there?) Were you there when they

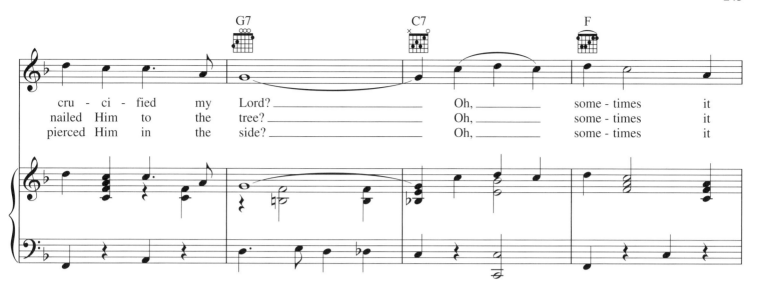

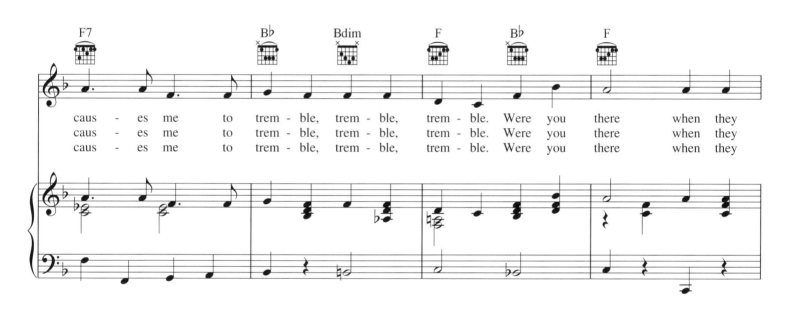

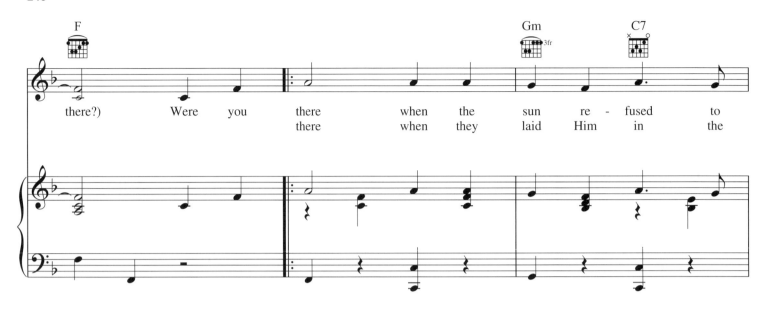

there?) Were you there when the sun re - fused to
there when when they laid Him in to the

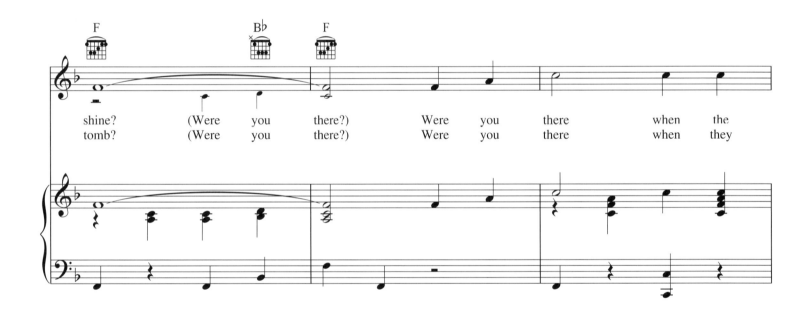

shine? (Were you there?) Were you there when the
tomb? (Were you there?) Were you there when they

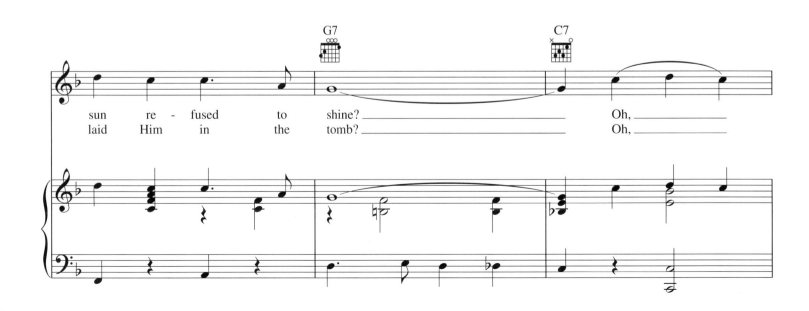

sun re - fused to shine? _____ Oh, _____
laid Him in to the tomb? _____ Oh, _____

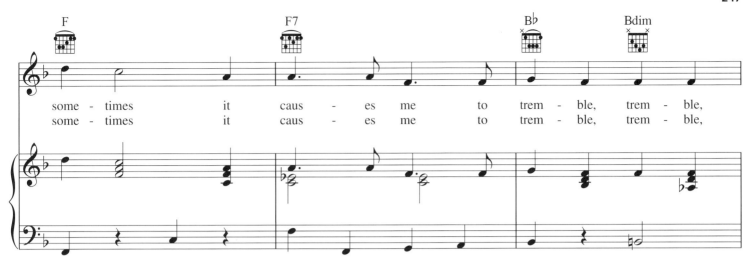

some - times it caus - es me to trem - ble, trem - ble,
some - times it caus - es me to trem - ble, trem - ble,

trem - ble. Were you there when the sun re - fused to
trem - ble. Were you there when they laid Him in to the

shine? _____ (Were you there?) Were you

tomb? _____ (Were you there?)

# WILL THE CIRCLE BE UNBROKEN

Words by ADA R. HABERSHON
Music by CHARLES H. GABRIEL

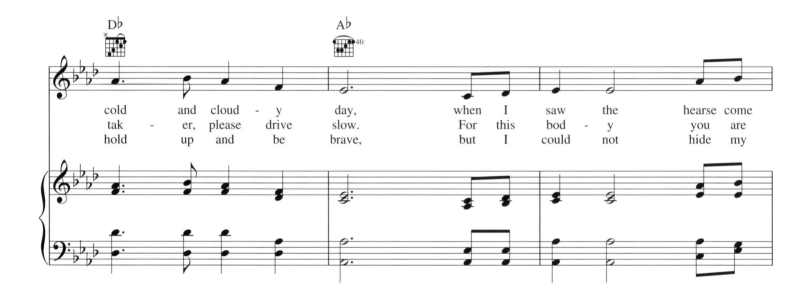

cir - cle    be   un - bro - ken,    by and  by,    Lord, by  and

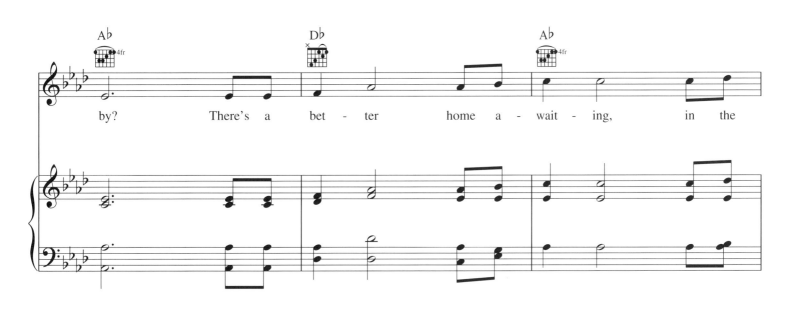

by?    There's a  bet - ter   home a - wait - ing,    in the

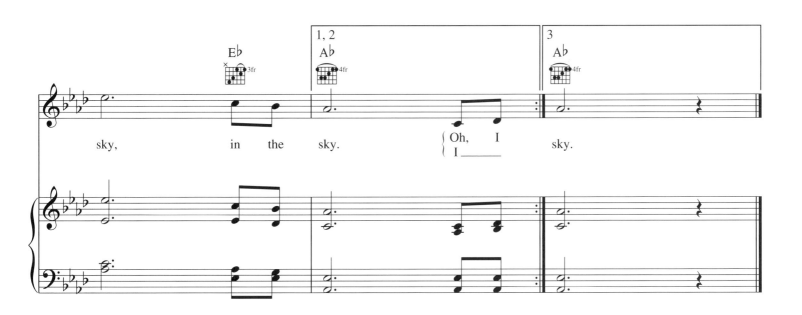

sky,    in the  sky.    Oh,  I    sky.
                        I _____

# WONDROUS LOVE

Southern American Folk Hymn

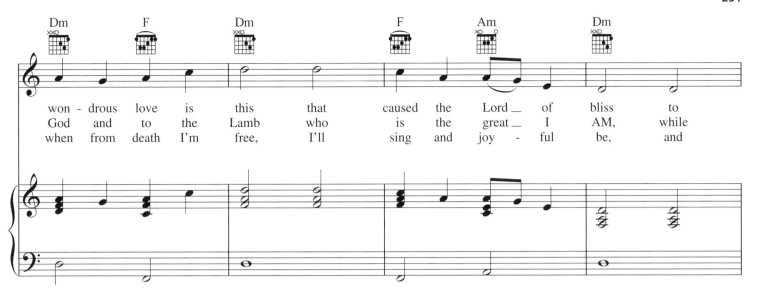

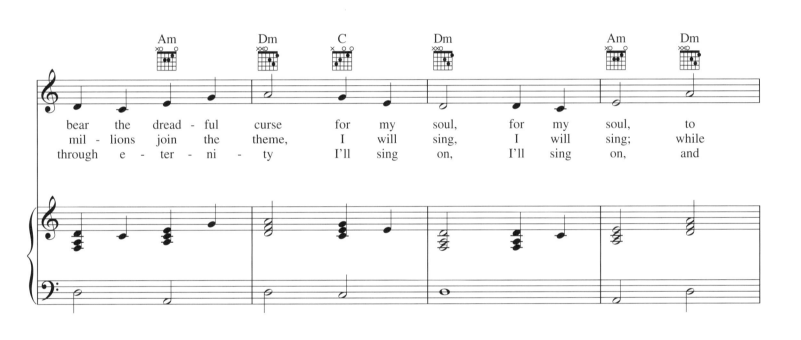

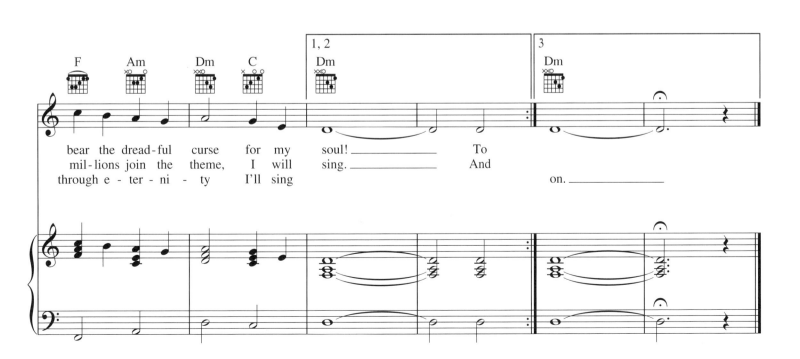

# YE BANKS AND BRAES O' BONNIE DOON

Words by ROBERT BURNS
Old Scottish Melody

# ZUM GALI GALI

Israeli Folksong

Zum ga-li, ga-li, ga-li, zum ga-li, ga-li.

Zum ga-li, ga-li, ga-li, zum ga-li, ga-li. He-cha-lutz le

*poco meno mosso*

# THE WILD ROVER

Irish Folksong

I've been a wild rov - er for man - y a
in - to an ale - house I used to a fre -
out of my pock - et I took sov - 'reigns

back to my par - ents, con - fess what I've

year, _____ and I've spent all my mon - ey on
quent, _____ and I told the land - la - dy my
bright, _____ and the land - la - dy's eyes o - pened
done, _____ and ask them to par - don their

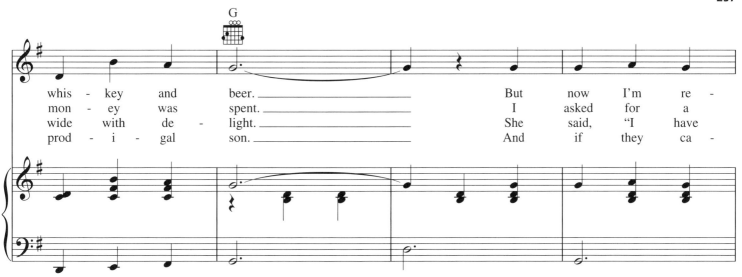

whis - key and beer._____ But now I'm re -
mon - ey was spent._____ I asked for a
wide with de - light._____ She said, "I have
prod - i - gal son._____ And if they ca -

turn - ing with gold in great store,_____ and I
bot - tle; she an - swered me, "Nay,_____ such a
whis - kies and wines of the best,_____ and the
ress me as oft - times be - fore,_____ then I

nev - er will play the wild rov - er no more.
cus - tom as yours I can get an - y day." And it's
words that I said, sure, were on - ly in jest."
nev - er will play the wild rov - er no more.

# Big Books of Music

*Our "Big Books" feature big selections of popular titles under one cover, perfect for performing musicians, music aficionados or the serious hobbyist. All books are arranged for piano, voice, and guitar, and feature stay-open binding, so the books lie flat without breaking the spine.*

**BIG BOOK OF BALLADS – 2ND ED.**
62 songs.
00310485 ..............................$19.95

**BIG BOOK OF BIG BAND HITS**
84 songs.
00310701 ..............................$22.99

**BIG BOOK OF BLUEGRASS SONGS**
70 songs.
00311484 ..............................$19.95

**BIG BOOK OF BLUES**
80 songs.
00311843 ..............................$19.99

**BIG BOOK OF BROADWAY**
70 songs.
00311658 ..............................$19.95

**BIG BOOK OF CHILDREN'S SONGS**
55 songs.
00359261 ..............................$16.99

**GREAT BIG BOOK OF CHILDREN'S SONGS**
76 songs.
00310002 ..............................$14.95

**FANTASTIC BIG BOOK OF CHILDREN'S SONGS**
66 songs.
00311062 ..............................$17.95

**MIGHTY BIG BOOK OF CHILDREN'S SONGS**
65 songs.
00310467 ..............................$14.95

**REALLY BIG BOOK OF CHILDREN'S SONGS**
63 songs.
00310372 ..............................$17.99

**BIG BOOK OF CHILDREN'S MOVIE SONGS**
66 songs.
00310731 ..............................$19.99

**BIG BOOK OF CHRISTMAS SONGS – 2ND ED.**
126 songs.
00311520 ..............................$19.95

**BIG BOOK OF CLASSIC ROCK**
77 songs.
00310801 ..............................$22.95

**BIG BOOK OF CLASSICAL MUSIC**
100 songs.
00310508 ..............................$19.99

**BIG BOOK OF CONTEMPORARY CHRISTIAN FAVORITES – 3RD ED.**
50 songs.
00312067 ..............................$21.99

**BIG BOOK OF COUNTRY MUSIC – 2ND ED.**
63 songs.
00310188 ..............................$19.95

**BIG BOOK OF COUNTRY ROCK**
64 songs.
00311748 ..............................$19.99

**BIG BOOK OF EARLY ROCK N' ROLL**
99 songs.
00310398 ..............................$19.95

**BIG BOOK OF '50S & '60S SWINGING SONGS**
67 songs.
00310982 ..............................$19.95

**BIG BOOK OF FOLK POP ROCK**
79 songs.
00311125 ..............................$24.95

**BIG BOOK OF FRENCH SONGS**
70 songs.
00311154 ..............................$19.95

**BIG BOOK OF GERMAN SONGS**
78 songs.
00311816 ..............................$19.99

**BIG BOOK OF GOSPEL SONGS**
100 songs.
00310604 ..............................$19.95

**BIG BOOK OF HYMNS**
125 hymns.
00310510 ..............................$17.95

**BIG BOOK OF IRISH SONGS**
76 songs.
00310981 ..............................$19.95

**BIG BOOK OF ITALIAN FAVORITES**
80 songs.
00311185 ..............................$19.99

**BIG BOOK OF JAZZ – 2ND ED.**
75 songs.
00311557 ..............................$19.95

**BIG BOOK OF LATIN AMERICAN SONGS**
89 songs.
00311562 ..............................$19.95

**BIG BOOK OF LOVE SONGS**
80 songs.
00310784 ..............................$19.95

**BIG BOOK OF MOTOWN**
84 songs.
00311061 ..............................$19.95

**BIG BOOK OF MOVIE MUSIC**
72 songs.
00311582 ..............................$19.95

**BIG BOOK OF NOSTALGIA**
158 songs.
00310004 ..............................$24.99

**BIG BOOK OF OLDIES**
73 songs.
00310756 ..............................$19.95

**BIG BOOK OF RAGTIME PIANO**
63 songs.
00311749 ..............................$19.95

**BIG BOOK OF RHYTHM & BLUES**
67 songs.
00310169 ..............................$19.95

**BIG BOOK OF ROCK**
78 songs.
00311566 ..............................$22.95

**BIG BOOK OF ROCK BALLADS**
67 songs.
00311839 ..............................$22.99

**BIG BOOK OF SOUL**
71 songs.
00310771 ..............................$19.95

**BIG BOOK OF STANDARDS**
86 songs.
00311667 ..............................$19.95

**BIG BOOK OF SWING**
84 songs.
00310359 ..............................$19.95

**BIG BOOK OF TORCH SONGS – 2ND ED.**
75 songs.
00310561 ..............................$19.99

**BIG BOOK OF TV THEME SONGS**
78 songs.
00310504 ..............................$19.95

**BIG BOOK OF WEDDING MUSIC**
77 songs.
00311567 ..............................$19.95

FOR MORE INFORMATION, SEE YOUR LOCAL MUSIC DEALER, OR WRITE TO:

**HAL•LEONARD® CORPORATION**
7777 W. BLUEMOUND RD. P.O. BOX 13819 MILWAUKEE, WI 53213

Prices, contents, and availability subject to change without notice.

Visit **www.halleonard.com**
for our entire catalog and to view our complete songlists.

1011

# HAL LEONARD COUNTRY DECADE SERIES

## THE 1950s

50 country golden oldies, including: Ballad of a Teenage Queen • Cold, Cold Heart • El Paso • Heartaches by the Number • Heartbreak Hotel • Hey, Good Lookin' • I Walk the Line • In the Jailhouse Now • Jambalaya (On the Bayou) • Sixteen Tons • Tennessee Waltz • Walkin' After Midnight • Your Cheatin' Heart • and more.
00311283 Piano/Vocal/Guitar .........................$15.99

## THE 1970s

41 songs, including: All the Gold in California • Coal Miner's Daughter • Country Bumpkin • The Devil Went to Georgia • The Gambler • Another Somebody Done Somebody Wrong Song • If We Make It Through December • Lucille • Sleeping Single in a Double Bed • and more.
00311285 Piano/Vocal/Guitar .........................$15.99

## THE 1980s

40 country standards, including: All My Ex's Live in Texas • The Chair • Could I Have This Dance • Coward of the County • Drivin' My Life Away • Elvira • Forever and Ever, Amen • God Bless the U.S.A. • He Stopped Loving Her Today • I Was Country When Country Wasn't Cool • Islands in the Stream • On the Road Again • Tennessee Flat Top Box • To All the Girls I've Loved Before • What's Forever For • You're the Reason God Made Oklahoma • and more.
00311282 Piano/Vocal/Guitar .........................$15.99

FOR MORE INFORMATION,
SEE YOUR LOCAL MUSIC DEALER,
OR WRITE TO:

## THE 1990s

40 songs, including: Achy Breaky Heart (Don't Tell My Heart) • Amazed • Blue • Boot Scootin' Boogie • Down at the Twist and Shout • Friends in Low Places • The Greatest Man I Never Knew • He Didn't Have to Be • Here's a Quarter (Call Someone Who Cares) • Man! I Feel like a Woman! • She Is His Only Need • Wide Open Spaces • You Had Me from Hello • You're Still the One • and more.
00311280 Piano/Vocal/Guitar .........................$16.95

## THE 2000s - 2nd Edition

35 contemporary country classics, including: Alcohol • American Soldier • Beer for My Horses • Blessed • Breathe • Have You Forgotten? • I Am a Man of Constant Sorrow • I Hope You Dance • I'm Gonna Miss Her (The Fishin' Song) • Long Black Train • No Shoes No Shirt (No Problems) • Redneck Woman • Where the Stars and Stripes and the Eagle Fly • Where Were You (When the World Stopped Turning) • and more.
00311281 Piano/Vocal/Guitar .........................$16.99

## HAL•LEONARD®
### CORPORATION
7777 W. BLUEMOUND RD. P.O. BOX 13819
MILWAUKEE, WISCONSIN 53213

Visit Hal Leonard online at
**www.halleonard.com**

Prices, contents and availability subject to change without notice.

0111